Inspired Remna[nts]
Curious Dreams
Mixed-Media Projects in Epoxy Clay

By Kerin Gale

NORTH LIGHT BOOKS
Cincinnati, Ohio

14 13 12 11 10   5 4 3 2 1

Distributed in Canada by Fraser Direct
100 Armstrong Avenue
Georgetown, ON, Canada L7G 5S4
Tel: (905) 877-4411

Distributed in the U.K. and Europe by F+W International
Brunel House, Newton Abbot, Devon, TQ12 4PU, England
Tel: (+44) 1626 323200, Fax: (+44) 1626 323319
E-mail: postmaster@davidandcharles.co.uk

Distributed in Australia by Capricorn Link
P.O. Box 704, S. Windsor, NSW 2756 Australia
Tel: (02) 4577-3555

Library of Congress Cataloging-in-Publication Data

Gale, Kerin.
  Inspired remnants / Kerin Gale.
    p. cm.
  Includes index.
  ISBN-13: 978-1-60061-944-1 (pbk. : alk. paper)
  1. Polymer clay craft. 2. Found objects (Art) I. Title.
TT297.G35 2011
745.57'2--dc22
                                    2010020199

Editors: Kristin Boys, Tonia Davenport
Designer: Corrie Schaffeld
Production Coordinator: Greg Nock
Photographers: Richard Deliantoni, Al Parrish, Christine Polomsky
Photo Stylist: Jan Nickum

www.fwmedia.com

Metric Conversion Chart

to convert	to	multiply by
Inches	Centimeters	2.54
Centimeters	Inches	0.4
Feet	Centimeters	30.5
Centimeters	Feet	0.03
Yards	Meters	0.9
Meters	Yards	1.1
Sq. Inches	Sq. Centimeters	6.45
Sq. Centimeters	Sq. Inches	0.16
Sq. Feet	Sq. Meters	0.09
Sq. Meters	Sq. Feet	10.8
Sq. Yards	Sq. Meters	0.8
Sq. Meters	Sq. Yards	1.2
Pounds	Kilograms	0.45
Kilograms	Pounds	2.2
Ounces	Grams	28.3
Grams	Ounces	0.035

Dedication

Lovingly dedicated to the Magnificent Ones—those daring to dream of creating the wondrous and unique—and to that exact moment when stepping back to see a masterpiece realized. Whether the masterpiece is a work of art or of your life, it matters not as long as you see it for what it is. It's all the same in the end.

Acknowledgments

For my family, husby and champion Charley Slaughter, pupsters and studio thrashers Solow and Hootie, my "kids" who are all grown up now (and quite well I might add!) Shawn, Sarah, Christine and Ben, you are all such amazing artists and are so cool you inspire me more than you know, my mom Martha Marie (yooo hoooo you!), my sister Donna who so patiently listens to my latest kooky ideas and doesn't say they are kooky, my other sister Diana who passed on but is still with me every day, her son Jim the Pinball Wizard, and all my extended family (even those of you who will never admit we're related (he he he)). Thanks for all your love, support and encouragement. OK, I am crying now so thanks also for the happy tears.

To Alicia Caudle of Altered Bits, who besides consistently ranking the highest on Google for "altered art" also ranks way up there for friendship, inspiration and an unending stash of the coolest ever found objects on her site.

To Jean Van Brederode, proprietor of CharmdImSur etsy shop and enamelist extraordinaire, thanks for befriending us and sharing the ride! It wouldn't be the same without you, Dear One.

To Maryann Ott who first told me about this magical clay so many years ago and encouraged me to try it.

To Erin and Amber at Aves Studio for their technical support, friendship and assistance. You rock. Your company rocks. And your clay is hard as a rock.

To Jerry at Silpak for even more technical support. Your magical silicone molds have helped me immensely and are used in so many projects in this book. It would be easy to fill several more books with things made from your awesome products. I'm really looking forward to experimenting more with them.

Most special thanks to Jenny Dill who without your help during the last frantic weeks of making works in progress this book would not have been finished in time. Your friendship and help came at the most perfect time. You are an answer to my prayers!

And to all members of the Mixed-Media Art ning site—it is a daily gift to see what you are all doing.

Contents

Curiously Inspired 7

Getting Started 8

Inspiring Projects 21

Resources 124

Index 126

Curiously Inspired

There was a time—not so long ago—when I was unable to separate myself from my art, and I dreaded anyone seeing it for fear they might not like it. Thankfully, those days are long gone. These days I find myself at ease, even when I receive less-than-enthusiastic reactions. In a way, it's actually an affirmation that I'm staying true to my artistic voice.

I first became aware that I had left my fearful-reaction days behind when I stopped off one day at my sister's house on my way back home from Artfest in Port Townsend, Washington. Diana had friends over that evening for dinner, and everyone wanted to see the class projects I made at the retreat. I laid them proudly on the table. They wandered over from the living room chatting excitedly about wanting to see what I'd made. As they reached the table, it suddenly became very quiet and they all just stared. There might as well have been dissected frogs laying there judging by their reactions. I couldn't help laughing because they thought my things were so odd. I told them not to worry since my things were definitely not for everyone.

It wasn't any one monumental thing that propelled me to the place where I am now—it was two things! The first was having someone I greatly admire as an artist tell me that I do good work. The second one was having epoxy clay in my studio (for more than ten years now) to help me actually make what my overactive imagination comes up with in any given week.

It has been quite a journey to make it to this place. I haven't forgotten what it felt like to struggle with letting anyone see what I'd made. Because of that feeling, I wanted to help others get past that and as fast as possible. So I did two things.

I started a ning group for mixed-media artists called—wait for it—MixedMediaArt.ning.com. The idea was to set up a place to share and learn in a supportive environment that helps others reach their artistic dreams. We celebrate accomplishments, have creative challenges and generally party online.

The second was writing this book so I could share as much as possible about the one art supply that helped me make the hurdle from being too shy to show anyone my art to wanting to share it with everyone and being completely OK if no one else liked it. If I help just one person get to that place, it all will have been worth it.

The potential here is nearly unlimited. What I'm trying to say (and this is a big claim, I know) is that what you are holding in your hands is the key to make nearly anything you can imagine. And it matters not if you are a sculptor or what your art experience has been up until now.

Imagine being able to build anything in three dimensions with "building blocks" that can go together in any configuration. Any design element that you find can be made into a mold, and then you can combine this with as many other elements as you'd like! Since it will hold itself and anything else together, now throw into the mix found objects, glass windows, moving parts, faux surface techniques such as rust, surface cracks and on and on. That doesn't leave much that you can't do, does it? And now, for a moment of silence while this sinks in . . .

Here are a few more examples of this clay's amazing properties:
- It is safe to use.
- It can be used in fish tanks and around other animals such as in zoo habitats.
- It's a perfect armature under polymer clay to make it stronger.
- It is a very strong adhesive.
- It is waterproof.
- It is very durable, even outside in extreme weather conditions.
- It can be used to attach disparate objects, as in found-object assemblage.
- It can be drilled, riveted, tapped and sanded.

To use it, you simply take equal parts of the clay and the hardener and mix them together. It slowly starts to cure, giving you a working time of about three hours, and after twenty-four hours it is very hard.

There is a wide range of projects in this book, but the focus for each is truly on the clay and its wonderful uses and options. There are plenty of books on beading, fiber art, sculpting clay and the like, so I will leave in-depth instruction for those categories to those books. Here, it's all about the clay, and I have plenty to share with you on that!

If you enjoy mixed-media art, I believe that as you start playing around with the projects in this book your imagination will begin to expand on some of the possibilities. It won't be long before your sense of adventure, if allowed to, will start to take over and then you, too, will experience the magic.

So let's get started!

Getting Started

It is highly recommended that you read through this chapter before doing any projects. Epoxy clay is simple to use, but there are some caveats and many helpful tips to be found here that you'll be thankful to know.

Tools and Materials

Epoxy Clay and Silicone—A Great Match!

As you can guess from the title, the main ingredient in making all of the projects in this book is the clay. So, what the heck is epoxy clay? It is a two-part art material—clay and hardener—in which equal amounts are mixed together. It's sold under several brand names and has many different formulas—some of which are toxic. There are two companies that sell most of the art-grade epoxy clay—Magic Sculp and Aves Studio. Aves Studio is my preferred supplier because in researching brands and formulas, I've found that it is the safest to use. Aves Studio doesn't call their clay "epoxy" because they wish to differentiate it from the other formulas available, so they use the name "Apoxie" instead. They have numerous formulas used for many applications—even taxidermy! In this book we'll focus on using only two of their formulas: Fixit Sculpt and Apoxie Sculpt.

Another product that is used extensively in this book also comes in two parts that are mixed together to activate— silicone rubber, which we'll use to create molds from all kinds of objects. Epoxy clay is perfect to use with these molds. There are far more companies making silicone rubber than I can possibly list here. I like to use Silputty formulas made by Silpak for several reasons. Silpak offers many kinds of silicone with different properties, they sell in large quantities (which is great for teaching workshops), and their staff is very helpful.

One of the main Silpak silicone formulas I use, Silputty 40, is somewhat toxic; however, it has a long cure (working) time, which is essential for making molds of larger objects. One frustrating thing about many silicone-mold formulas is that they can set up before you are done trying to get your impression. So, for me, it is worth it to be able to make the larger molds with a putty consistency. You can bet if a safer, less-toxic formula comes out that has a long setup time, I'll be using that one!

There are more fluid types of silicone that can be applied to your object with a brush, but, as a beginner, you probably want to start with putty formulas that mix together just like the epoxy clay. Please note that, in actuality, there are numerous types of rubber mixtures, and they cure in various ways, so it can get a bit confusing. For our purposes, whatever brand you use, you'll want to use RTV (Room Temperature Vulcanizing) two-part silicone putty— preferably one where you mix equal parts of A and B together. It's also the official silicone putty of the planet Vulcan—Live Long and Prosper.

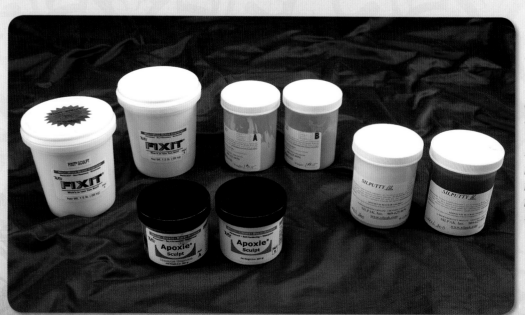

From left to right: Aves Studio Fixit Sculpt Part A and B (epoxy clay), Silpak Silputty 40 Part A and B, Silpak Silputty BR Part A and B, Aves Studio Apoxie Sculpt Part A and B

Note: We will use all these products in the book at some point, but by far most of the projects will be made with Fixit Sculpt and Silputty 40.

Other Materials

Some other items you'll want to have on hand to have fun with the projects in this book include:

- Alcohol inks
- Powdered pigments
- Collage (acrylic gel) medium—matte and clear gloss
- Acrylic paints
- Disposable baby wipes
- Hand lotion

Tools

- Magnification visors (highly recommended for detail work!)
- Heat gun
- Ruler
- Silicone-tipped clay shaper
- Clay cleanup tool with sharp blade
- Handheld drill
- Paintbrushes
- Small scissors
- Tweezers
- Needle-nose pliers
- Wire cutters

Getting to Know Epoxy Clay

Here are some tips to keep in mind while you begin to use the clay:

- In order to use the clay, it must first be mixed together. (Equal parts are mixed thoroughly.)
- It hardens by a chemical process, so it "cures" rather than "dries."
- The clay is a very strong adhesive and sticks to itself and almost everything else except silicone.
- Heat accelerates the time it takes to cure. This heat includes applying friction (mixing). So the longer you mix the clay, the faster it will cure. You can also pop it in your craft/toaster oven by itself or inside a silicone mold. Very low temperatures are recommended. Preheat your oven, turn it off and allow to cool to around 150 degrees. As with polymer clay, use proper ventilation. Check after five minutes. Once fully cured, it can handle higher temps such as when using as an armature under polymer clay. You can also use a heat gun.
- Conversely, the clay does not cure as fast in cold temperatures. It can be placed in the freezer to delay curing—even if it is frozen solid, it will thaw and be workable for several hours longer than if you hadn't frozen it. Note that the clay will continue curing when frozen, just not as fast. (And be careful not to glue the clay to your freezer!)

Quickie Definitions

Mold: Cured silicone with the shape of your object
Casting: Clay that has come from the mold
Squee: The involuntary sound made when you realize how cool this clay is

Tips for Working With Mixed Clay

- Use hand lotion or Liquid Gloves before handling or mixing. If the clay tends to stick to your hands use lots of lotion (any inexpensive one is fine). Even lathering the lotion on several times while mixing will not impede the curing of the clay. It will slightly change the surface to become shinier, but that is the only difference I've noticed. Also, stretching the clay will make it seem stickier than compressing it will.
- Let the clay rest for a few minutes after mixing. Place on a nonstick surface (silicone craft sheet or the back of a silicone mold).
- Wipe the clay from your hands and tools often with alcohol-based disposable wipes. (Using these wipes to remove the clay before actually washing your hands in the sink will help prevent your drain from clogging.) Keep these handy; you will love how great they work to clean up the clay (also good for resin too). If you happen to have an alcohol-free formula, you can add rubbing alcohol to them.
- If you forget to wipe uncured clay from your tools when you're done using them, you can usually remove any buildup with drywall sanding screen.
- If the clay becomes difficult to remove from the container, it can be microwaved for a few seconds at a time to soften the clay.
- If you are working on a multi-step project, you can mix up a larger volume of clay and put some aside in the refrigerator or freezer to delay the cure time. Remember that since this is a chemical process, the clay will still cure rock hard, even in the freezer, and will be fully cured in about twenty-four hours.

9

States of Clay

This chart will help you make the best use of the clay from a raw (unmixed) state through when you first mix it and on to when it becomes fully cured and rock hard. For example, when it's first mixed, it's very sticky and becomes less sticky as it cures. So if you want to use it as a glue, you wouldn't use clay that had been mixed an hour ago.

State	Purpose	Notes
Unmixed	Fixit Sculpt Part A is excellent to use for propping up work in progress. If your pieces are unusual shapes it may be difficult to hold them in a vise, etc. The uncured clay will accommodate any shape.	Unmixed clay touching mixed clay will not affect the final piece but it may need to be cleaned off. You may want to tint some unmixed clay so as not to get it confused with the other clay. I recommend testing unmixed clay in an inconspicuous area to make sure it doesn't affect the finish of whatever you are working with.
Mixed—first 20 to 30 minutes	Adhesive	It will stick to anything that isn't silicone including you, your table and your tools. In a pinch, you can set the mixed clay temporarily on a wet disposable wipe, and it most likely won't stick. But as the wipe begins to dry, the clay will start to adhere to the wipe.
Malleable 30 to 60 minutes	Shape altering	A clay casting that is beginning to set up can be removed from the mold and "sculpted" to change the shape while still retaining the details from the mold. For example, you have made a mold of a bird that has a curved tail looking straight ahead. You can remove the clay bird from the mold and make its head look down and straighten the tail up instead.
Cured 3 to 4 hours	Very hard	It can be drilled, sanded or tapped (adding threads for bolts or screws to be attached).

The Unbreakable Comb

A friend told me that when he was in grade school a classmate had brought an "unbreakable comb" and was showing it to the class. He wanted to see for himself so he took the comb and snapped it in half. This same thing happened with another friend of mine. She was showing samples of things she'd made with epoxy clay and how strong it was. Yes, you guessed it. A man took one of her pieces and snapped it in two.

I mention this because while the clay is very strong, it isn't unbreakable. We know glass is strong and works very well to hold beverages, but you wouldn't grab the stem of a wine glass and try to snap it in half. (If you ever do, it can be repaired with epoxy clay!)

Cured Versus Dried

Why does it matter if you know that the clay "cures" rather than "dries"? For one thing, it means you can cure the clay under water! So if you ever find yourself in the position that a student of mine did, with a leaking metal pan under her air conditioner that was full of water and dripping down from the attic, you will be set. Just fill the hole up with clay! For another thing, it helps to understand what makes the clay set up so that you can make this work in your favor rather than against you. If you introduce heat to mixed clay that is in the process of curing, it becomes much softer and "gooey." This might make you think that it is actually getting sticky again and can be used as an adhesive. But what will actually happen is as soon as you remove it from the heat and let it begin to cool, it will set up much faster than it would otherwise. This is because, like liquid transparent resin, it cures faster with heat and slower when cool or cold.

Mixing Clay

Amounts of Clay to Mix

This clay goes a lot farther than you'd guess, so here are some guidelines on how much to mix.

- Pea size—this is normally the smallest size you will mix. Visualize two peas (one of Part A and one of Part B) and when you have the two pea size balls, mix them together. This is perfect for touching up little areas.

- Grape size—Surprisingly, this amount of clay will go a very long way, especially when working on jewelry-size projects. It is much more cost effective to mix up additional clay if you need it, than to mix too much initially, as there is no way to save it once it is mixed.

- Golf-ball size—This is about as much as you'd ever need to mix unless your project is huge. Even then you'd likely want to mix up the clay as you are ready for it since it will easily stick to itself after it is cured, enabling you to build very large pieces.

1. Start by making two balls of the same size, one of Part A and one of Part B.

2. Then flatten out the two balls and layer them together.

3. Fold the stack in half and press the layers together.

4. Fold in half a second time, flattening and pressing the layers together.

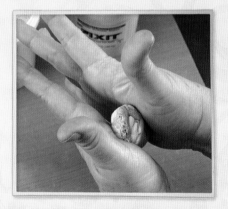

5. Roll the clay into a ball between your palms (don't use fingertips).

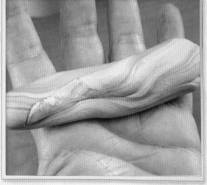

6. Work the clay into the start of a snake shape. Fold it in half and repeat rolling process several times.

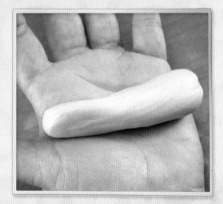

7. When it has become consistent in color, it is thoroughly mixed.

11

Making and Using Molds

A few thoughts if you're feeling sheepish about the cloning process. What if you don't have the heart to use something that is rare on a piece—especially a piece you'll never see again after you sell it? This is when molds can become your best friend. Especially when you can learn to make very convincing copies using patinas and other aging techniques. Working with the clay castings, combining them with other objects and/or other castings is a fun and playful way to get a feel for how to work with the clay.

Making a Basic One-Sided Mold

1. Before you begin, put on non-latex gloves. Mix the two parts of the silicone putty according to the manufacturer's instructions. In order to mix them together faster, use the same method you use to mix the epoxy.

2. Mix the silicone until it reaches a solid color. Flatten and shape the silicone into a piece that is slightly larger than your object and approximately ¼" (6mm) thick.

3. Shape the mixed mold material in roughly the same shape as the object to copy. Place the silicone over to one side of the piece, and slowly and lightly press down over the surface one section at a time so as not to trap air bubbles. Once you have placed it down, leave it.

4. Allow the silicone to cure for about 15–20 minutes. Once the silicone has started to cure, you no longer need to wear gloves to work with it.

5. You can check if the silicone has fully cured, by making an imprint with your fingernail. If it leaves a mark, the silicone has not yet cured.

6. When the silicone has cured, gently bend back the mold (it will be flexible).

Silicone Savvy

- Sometimes the mold material can alter the appearance of an item, so before beginning to make a mold of a cherished item, test a small section in an inconspicuous place with a tiny bit of mixed silicone putty.

- Once the silicone is in place don't attempt to move or remove it until it is cured. Think: uncured = sticky and messy, cured = completely nonstick.
- If your piece is rare, sentimental or expensive, I'd recommend you not make a mold of it because you'd risk damaging it in the process.

12

Inspired Tip

Use the freshest clay (recently mixed) on detailed molds for best results.

Materials

mixed epoxy clay
silicone mold
water or disposable wipe

Making a Basic One-Sided Mold

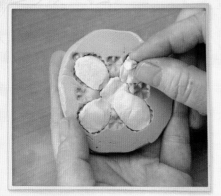

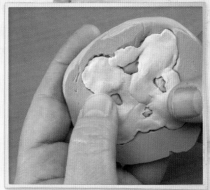

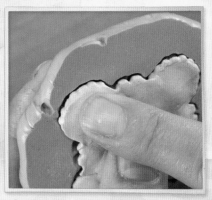

1. Press a small batch of mixed clay into the mold. It helps to add small sections at a time. Compress the clay rather than stretch it for best results.

2. Rub the exposed clay firmly with a disposable wipe or a moderately wet finger to smooth it. (Don't "flood" the clay with so much water that it seeps into the mold.) Also be careful of where you fill the mold; you want to fill just the areas in which you want clay. In this example, there is "negative" space in the clay. See the example below for the best ways to fill a mold.

3. Pull the clay back slightly away from all the edges of the mold with the tip of your finger. This is a very important and often overlooked step. If you don't, your clay casting will look like, well, a clay casting. Pulling the clay back from the edges of the mold will make it look like the object itself. This is what is meant by the "Better" example below. Allow the clay to cure for at least 30 minutes before trying to remove it until you gain experience. Many times I can remove the clay immediately, but it took a while to get the feel for how to do this.

Best Method for Filling a Mold

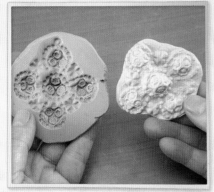

GOOD

No matter how you fill a mold, you are going to get a nicely shaped imprint in your clay. However, pressing one big mound of clay into the mold will result in a finished product that looks exactly like what it is—a piece of clay that was pressed in a mold, rather than a "real" object.

BETTER

To get a nice, realistic look for your clay, be aware of where the edges are. After the mold is filled, pull back the clay from the edges as shown above in step 3.

BEST

For the best, most realistic results, be aware of any negative space in a mold, such as in this object here, and don't press clay over those areas.

Making a Mold for Smoother Surfaces

The regular two-part RTV silicone molding putty that we've been using so far works great for most objects. However, sometimes a super smooth surface is preferable, such as when you want to make very convincing copies of vintage sandwich glass or antique crystals. This is accomplished by using a two-part silicone molding *paste* instead of a putty. The following method that I developed will save a lot of time over the conventional methods of applying multiple layers of silicone pastes.

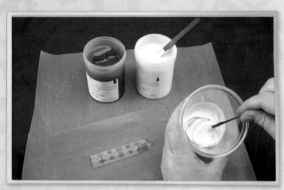

1. Place your item on a nonstick craft sheet. Add equal amounts of part A and B into a disposable mixing cup. Add part A first since it is thinner and more easily mixed from the bottom of the cup. Using a craft stick, mix the parts together slowly to avoid introducing air bubbles. Slowly pour the mixture into another cup using the craft stick as a spatula to remove as much as possible. The paste that was up against the sides and on the bottom is now in the middle of the second cup so it can be thoroughly mixed.

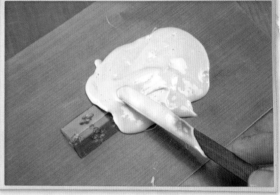

2. When the paste mixture is a consistent color, spread it over your crystal (or similar object), using a craft stick. Allow the paste to cure thoroughly (about 30 to 40 minutes).

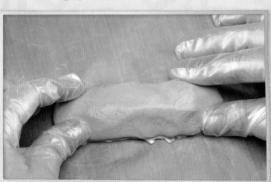

3. At this point, traditional methods would call for mixing up several more batches of paste and allowing each thin layer to cure before applying the next, which could easily take half a day or more. Forget about that! Pick up the mold and the crystal together and trim the excess silicone paste around the crystal with scissors leaving about a ¼" (6mm) border. Place the crystal down on the craft sheet.

Mix some silicone molding putty and place it over the layer of paste silicone. Press the putty firmly around the paste so that it forms a second layer extending out about ¼" (6mm) from the edge of the crystal. Allow to fully cure before removing the crystal from the mold.

4. To begin casting with the mold, place some uncured epoxy clay on the craft sheet and press the mold right side up into the clay. Adjust the mold as needed so that it is level. Following the manufacturer's directions, mix ICE resin and pour into the mold. If the item you created a mold from was very deep, consider using two or more layers of resin, allowing each to cure before adding a new layer. Wipe away any spillage with a disposable wipe. Allow the resin layer(s) to fully cure and remove the hardened resin by bending the mold back gently.

14

Repairing Molded Clay

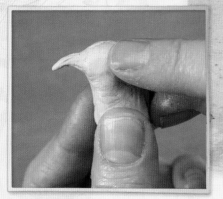 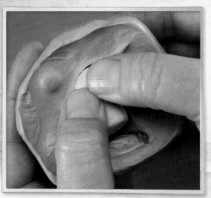 

1. If you find that a part of your molded clay is missing or damaged, you can fix it. Just place a thin layer of mixed, uncured clay over the area to which you want to add the element.

2. Place the clay piece back into the mold and pinch down firmly to create a new imprint.

3. Allow the new clay to cure. Voilà! Now you have a perfect piece.

Repairing Missing or Damaged Texture

In the example above, the bird head was relatively smooth, and the seam could be blended somewhat easily. But what if you need to repair a heavily textured surface? In this technique we use two steps to blend the clay. We use a very thin layer just as before but thick enough to fill the hole and bring the clay level up with the rest of the casting.

1. Note the concave area near the point of the clay shaper tool. This is what needs to be repaired.

2. Place a thin piece of uncured clay over the missing/damaged texture. (Clay tool used as a pointer.)

3. Press the clay casting into the mold and press firmly in the area where the hole has been patched. You do not need to worry about the old and new texture lining up exactly as your eye will fill in the lines. Remove the casting from the mold. (Note: If the mold itself has the imperfection, you can flip the casting around and use the other side of the mold.)

non-latex gloves

silicone molding putty

object from which you'll create mold

nonstick craft mat

paintbrush or dowel

petroleum jelly

Making Double-Sided, 3-D Molds

1. Form mixed silicone putty to fit the original item with at least a ½" (13mm) border all around and working on a nonstick sheet, press the front of the object into the silicone.

2. Poke a few holes in the mold using the end of a paintbrush (or similar object). These will act as "registration marks" for the two halves of the mold.

3. Brush petroleum jelly on the surface of the mold to prevent the other half of the mold from sticking to it.

Using the Double-Sided Mold

To sculpt clay using the mold, fill each half as you would a basic flat mold, making sure that each half is completely filled. Then press the halves together, aligning the registration "pegs" and holes. Check to see how the casting looks. Add or remove clay as needed to completely fill it up with clay but not so much that clay is seeping out the sides.

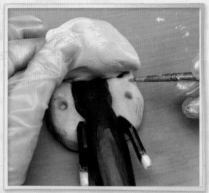

4. After the first half of the mold has cured, mix and shape more silicone for the other half of the mold. Place it over the back of the object as it sits in the first half of the mold. Press the mixed silicone compound over the object and the other mold half, pressing at the sides to ensure it works itself into the holes. When the other half is fully cured, remove it.

5. Finally, remove the original object from the mold.

Cleaning the Edges of a Molded 3-D Piece

Materials

cured clay casting
(molded from a double-
sided mold)

craft knife
disposable wipe
drywall screen

1. Clay pieces cast from a mold with two halves will have a seam where the two halves of the mold matched up. To clean it up, start by removing the extra clay, using a craft knife.

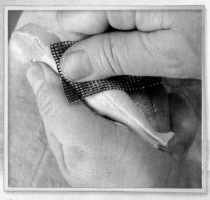

2. Place a moist, disposable wipe on your work surface to catch sanding dust as you work. Use a small piece of drywall screen to sand the edges smooth.

3. Add a thin layer of mixed clay to the seam (using a bit of water on your finger or a disposable wipe, if necessary). Allow the new clay to cure.

Creating Texture Tools

Sometimes you simply want to add some texture to clay without molding an entire piece. You can craft your own texture tools to have on hand for adding texture. I recommend making a small tool for getting into small spaces and a larger tool (or a flat texture sheet) for covering larger areas.

Materials

mixed clay
18-gauge
(approximately) wire
wire cutters

silicone molding
putty
objects to use for
creating texture

1. Create a short snake shape from a piece of mixed clay. Work the clay around a short length of wire and also flay one end of the clay. Trim the excess wire and allow the piece to cure. This will form the handle and an area for which to connect the silicone.

2. Mix a small amount of silicone molding compound according to the package instructions. Press the ball of compound onto the flayed end of the cured clay handle.

3. Press or "stamp" the silicone onto an object with texture. Allow the silicone to cure, then remove the mold from the object. Here we are making an impression from a design on the knife handle.

Materials

chipboard shape
mixed clay
nonstick craft sheet

Creating Challenging Shapes

It can be pretty tricky to create perfectly straight lines and other precise shapes, by hand, in clay. In comes chipboard to the rescue! Chipboard is easy to cut to any shape and can take any amount of heat that you'd use in the rapid cure techniques you've already learned. The chipboard gets completely covered in clay, so the best part is that everyone will wonder how you suddenly got SO good!

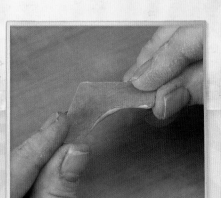

1. After you have cut your desired shape, place the chipboard shape on a non-stick craft sheet. Shape a thin piece of mixed clay to match the shape of the chipboard, and apply the clay to the chipboard. Smooth the clay evenly over the surface, using just a partial drop of water to curve the clay around the edges. Let the clay cure.

2. Repeat the application of clay on the other side of the chipboard, using a slightly larger piece of clay to give you a bit extra to wrap around the edges.

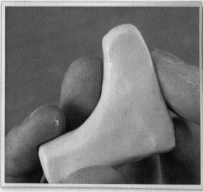

3. Blend the front and the back layers together to hide the chipboard.

Inspired Tip

If you only want the texture on one side of the chipboard, put a thin layer of clay on the back side. (This will prevent warping.) This works just like applying counter enamel on the back of a piece of enameled jewelry so I call it "counter clay." Then add whatever you'd like to the front side.

4. Reinforce the curved lines with your finger and the straight lines by pressing down gently on a flat surface.

5. Smooth out any final areas where needed and leave to cure.

Creating a Faux Aged Finish

I've discovered several recipes for aged finishes by combining commonly used supplies. This is one of my favorites. Try experimenting with mixing the "big three" materials (alcohol ink, acrylic paint and weathering powder) in different ways and then removing some of the previous layers.

Materials

alcohol ink: Espresso (Adirondak)

acrylic paint: Burnt Umber Light (Golden)

nonstick craft sheet to act as a palette

cured clay piece

paintbrushes

disposable wipe

weathering powder: Dirty Brown (Doc O'Brien's)

medium or fine sandpaper

acrylic glazing medium or white craft glue

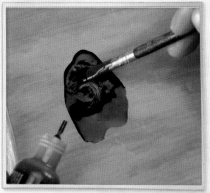

1. Mix together a small amount of ink and paint. You can do this directly on a nonstick craft sheet if you like.

2. "Scrub" the mixture onto the surface of the clay, working it into the recesses with the paintbrush.

3. Remove some of the mixture from the surface using a disposable wipe.

4. Brush on additional alcohol ink.

5. Add weathering powder to the surface. Remove some of the mixture from the surface using a disposable wipe. Sand some of the surface using sandpaper, as well.

6. Then, brush on a mixture of powder and acrylic medium. Remove some of the mixture from the surface using a disposable wipe. Allow to dry.

Inspiring Projects

*A*re you eager to test-drive this clay for yourself and make one of the projects? If you'd like to make something simpler to start with, we've arranged the projects from easier to more difficult. As you work through the steps of these projects, you'll start to learn the subtle nuances of how this remarkable art material behaves. So take your time, enjoy the process and have some patience—especially at first. Since this is the first book about epoxy clay, realize that I've barely scratched the surface of the possibilities. This means that YOU are now a trailblazer! Keeping notes about ideas that you want to experiment with just may result in exciting new techniques. Perhaps you will be the one to write the second book about epoxy clay! I feel like I'm nudging little birdies from the nest, and now they will not just fly but soar. I'm so excited to see what you do with this!

Sailor's Valentine
Devoted Gift

Oh, if it be to choose and call thee mine, love, thou art every day my Valentine.

—Thomas Hood

Sailors' valentines were popular in the 1800s and a lucky lass would receive one of them as a souvenir from her beloved sailor's travels. Although it is a very romantic notion to envision a sailor making one of these to while away the long hours spent at sea, most of these intricate pieces made from many kinds of shells were purchased at various ports. Original antique sailors' valentines are becoming quite collectable, while newer versions remain for sale today at many nautical gift shops.

I've always loved mosaics but for some reason felt a bit intimidated by the grouting process. But working with the epoxy clay as a substitute for grout couldn't be easier! You don't need to clean up afterwards—just simply press the elements down into the clay and

the next day it will be as if they were set in stone. While this project uses shells, it would be quite easy to use this process for other mosaic projects, such as a mirror, picture frame or a jewelry box. Not only that, but epoxy clay is even sturdier than the grout used in traditional mosaics.

I've meant for this project to be framed with a traditional curved-glass lens. Determine if you'd like the project to use the same. If so, try thinking outside the box. I used parts from a vintage alarm clock to get curved glass and frame. But you can still complete the project if you choose not to frame the piece. Using chipboard allows for the creation of a mosaic in any shape or size, so regardless of whether you use a frame or not, you can let your imagination rule.

Materials

- nonstick craft sheet
- pencil
- chipboard
- craft knife
- round frame (or clock) with glass
- ruler

- printout or photocopy of a vintage photo
- découpage medium
- paintbrushes
- acrylic paint (to match the background of your photo)
- unmixed epoxy clay

- towel
- shells in assorted sizes
- Diamond Glaze or clear resin
- disposable wipe
- gold metallic paint
- gold leaf

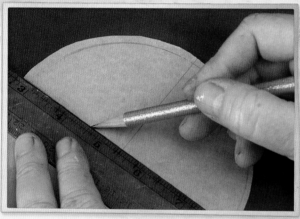

1. Draw the shape of the frame (or shape of your choice if not using a frame) on the chipboard and cut out. If using a frame, make sure that the chipboard fits comfortably inside the frame. Then, determine how much of the chipboard shape extends beyond the viewable area inside the frame. Draw a line to mark where this is so that you don't apply the mosaic pieces beyond that line. Divide the shape into four quadrants.

2. Cut out the vintage photo. Apply découpage medium to the area on the chipboard where the image will be placed. Brush on the medium in an area slightly larger than the image so that the edges will be fully adhered. Apply more découpage medium over the top of the image and let it dry. Apply a second coat to seal in the image.

3. If the vintage image does not have a large enough border for your liking, you can "extend" the border by painting around the photo with acrylic paint and blending the paint into the photocopy. I use my finger for this. Allow the paint to dry thoroughly.

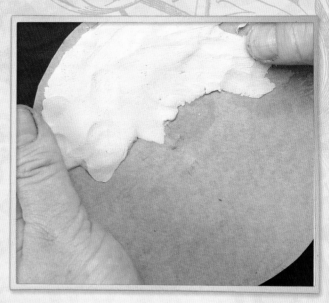

4. In pencil, sketch around the image on the chipboard to create sections for the seashell mosaic. Traditional sailors' valentines used geometric shapes, which looked cool filled in with shells of contrasting colors and shapes. If you want to buck tradition, feel free to use free-flowing shapes and curved lines to create your sections.

5. Flip the chipboard over and apply a thin layer of mixed, uncured clay to act as a "counter-clay" (see Inspired Tip on page 18). Having this on the back will keep the front from warping when you begin adding clay and shells to it. Note that the clay doesn't need to go all the way to the edge; as long as it covers most of the back, the chipboard will not warp. Allow to cure or flip it back over, but keep it on a nonstick surface.

6. Lay out the elements you'd like to use on your mosaic to get a sense of placement. Then, start with one of the sections around the center image, and mix a pea-size amount of clay. Form the clay to roughly the shape of the section and make it about 1/16" (2mm) thick. Press it onto the chipboard.

7. Using a craft knife, cut off any clay that extends beyond the border line for that section. The clay should be right on the line so it meets up with the other sections with no gaps in between. Remove the excess clay and set aside. Depending on how long the clay has been allowed to cure, the edges may become jagged after cutting. If that happens, smooth the clay with just a bit of water. Blot with a towel to absorb any excess water.

8. Gently press a shell (or other object) into the clay far enough so it is partially embedded in the clay. (Remember that the clay is an adhesive so you don't have to press it in all the way for it to adhere.) The idea is to push each shell down a little bit but not so far that the section of clay is distorted too much. Continue filling the section with shells. Use a craft knife or tweezers to align shells along the edges of the section, if needed.

9. Place the curved glass piece and frame over the shells to make sure they still fit together. If not, adjust the shells until all the pieces fit. Repeat steps 6–8 to fill in the rest of the sections with different pieces. If using triangular-shaped shells, like the purple ones I used here, start from the outer edge and work your way toward the center. If you like a certain color shell but it doesn't fit the way you'd like, consider smashing the shells to get smaller pieces. Also, remember that the sections should butt against each other with no gaps in between (but they should not overlap).

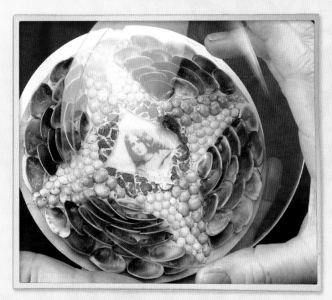

10. Apply embellishments, such as a seahorse or starfish, with a tiny bit of fresh clay. Fill in the area over the image with Diamond Glaze or resin. Place the shell mosaic onto the clock face as a backing. Carefully place the curved glass piece over the shell mosaic.

11. While holding the pieces in place, apply clay around the outside to bond the pieces together, and clean up any excess off the metal frame with a disposable wipe. Allow to cure and paint the clay with gold metallic paint and/ or cover with gold leaf to match the frame.

Entwined Hearts
Magnetic Pendant

"With you I'm not shy to show the way I feel
With you I might try my secrets to reveal
for you are a magnet and I am steel"

—Walter Egan
from the song "Magnet and Steel"

The secret in these hearts are magnets! Only one heart is actually attached to the necklace. The other one stays because of magnet love. If you think of all the possibilities of things that can be made with magnets, this will open up so many opportunities if you let your imagination lead you. For example, just off the top of my head . . .

how about a pendant with a heart shape with another heart that fits inside? Or keys that fit into a lock and will stay there? Maybe two sides to a heart that when brought near each other will become as one? What about more whimsical things like a carrot that sticks on a bunny? And on and on.

We'll also use reclaimed twisted copper jewelry wire and embed part of it in the clay to create unique bales for hanging. One source for this wire is the wire trees with little beads that were so popular in the 1970s. They can be found at thrift stores quite often. Then more of the wire is wrapped randomly around the heart to enhance the "entwined" feel.

Materials

unmixed epoxy clay

nonstick craft sheet

small, super strong magnets, 2

reclaimed twisted copper wire

small decorative element mold (to provide texture)

acrylic paints: Quinacridone, Nickel/Azo Gold, Quinacridone Crimson (Golden)

alcohol ink: Cranberry (Adirondak)

paintbrushes

Anita's Fragile Crackle medium

acrylic varnish

reclaimed chain

disposable wipes

1. Sculpt clay free-form into a somewhat flat (¼" [6mm] thick) heart.

2. Place a small, round magnet in the center of the heart. Add uncured clay to the top of the magnet to secure it. Repeat steps 1–2 to sculpt a smaller heart that fits on top of the larger heart.

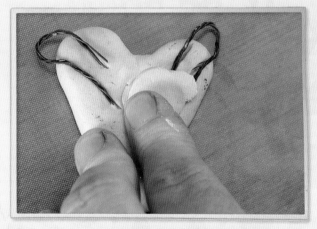

3. While the clay is still fresh, embed a loop of twisted wire on either side of the large heart. Smooth the clay over the top of the wire to secure. Allow the clay to cure so the magnet and wire are secured.

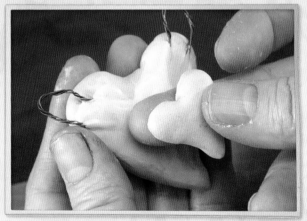

4. Determine the front and back of the smaller heart. Keeping your finger between the hearts, check for the correct magnetic pull without allowing the hearts to touch yet. (After the clay is cured the magnets will be secure and the hearts will be held together.)

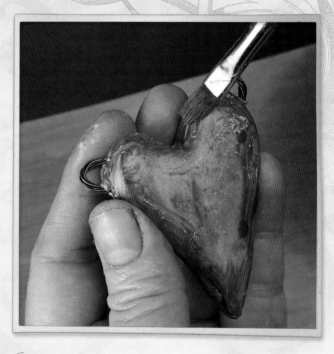

5. Add texture to the front of the smaller heart using a texture mold. (You can use multiple texture molds to combine textures to give the piece more depth.)

6. Apply color to the large heart, using a mixture of acrylic paint and alcohol inks, with a paintbrush.

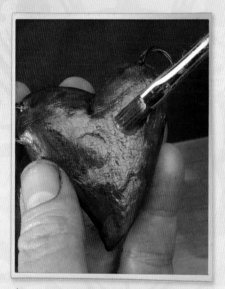

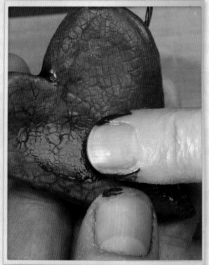

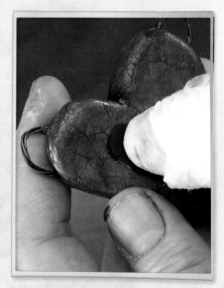

7. Apply crackle paint to the larger heart following the manufacturer's directions.

8. When the crackle layer is dry, rub in darker paint to bring out the crackle texture. Allow the paint to sit on the surface for a few moments.

9. Wipe away the excess paint with a disposable wipe. Repeat the process to force the darker paint down in the crackled areas, if necessary.

10. Seal both hearts with several layers of matte acrylic varnish allowing each layer to dry thoroughly in between coats. Wrap the larger heart with aged twisted copper wire, circling the heart once or twice.

11. Place the little heart near the large heart, and it will stay magnetically attached to the front. Attach chain and jewelry findings, as you like, to finish.

From the Gallery

The Empress
Alicia Caudle

A small shrine dedicated to The Empress—the third card in the tarot deck. All elements are attached using Aves Fixit Sculpt.

5" x 7" x 2¹/₂"

Lion's Paw
Necklace

Only in art will the lion lie down with the lamb, and the rose grow without thorn.

Martin Amis

Ever since I discovered Keith LoBue's amazing work, I've been fascinated with unique ways to finish off a necklace. My good friend, Jenny Dill, who helped me with many of the works in progress for this book, brought over a magazine she had just purchased. In it was a reprint of an article about Keith with some photos of his jewelry. I skimmed through the article and showed Jenny a piece called Water Cure and told her that I owned that one. She, of course, didn't believe me until I brought it out to the studio to show her. Don't you just love such moments! Anyway, Water Cure is connected with a key that he cut in half and used the barrel end to interlock with the top. How clever is that!

And with the versatility of epoxy clay, now there are a kazillion more possibilities to discover your own signature findings. The ability to embed wire into the clay opens up so many possibilities and here is just one.

This project is really fun since the clasp is part of the design and isn't really obvious at first glance. It's also easier to unhook a piece from the front rather than the back. Thinking about the found objects that you might have on hand right now and what you might do with them using the techniques in this project just may give you some unique designs.

Materials

unmixed epoxy clay

lion's paw silicone mold

nonstick craft sheet

19-gauge wire

wire cutters

chain-nose pliers

hammer

steel bench block

round-nose pliers

found-object focal piece that can act as a clasp for a wire hook (a ring shape works well)

acrylic paint: Burnt Umber (Golden)

paintbrushes

alcohol ink: Espresso (Adirondak)

metallic powder: Pewter (Pearl Ex)

acrylic varnish

chain and jump rings

1. Mix up a small amount of epoxy clay. Make a casting of a lion's paw (or similar arm/hand shape) using mixed epoxy clay. Before the clay is fully cured and still pliable, carefully remove it from the mold.

2. Lay the casting face up on a nonstick craft sheet and bend it into a curved shape. Make a second casting, but this time, curve it in the opposite direction. Compare the two castings and adjust them if necessary so they appear symmetrical. Allow both to fully cure.

3. Bend a 4" (10cm) length of 19-gauge wire in half. Flare out the last ¼" (6mm) of each end—just slightly, using chain-nose pliers.

4. Flatten the wire with a hammer on a steel bench block or anvil.

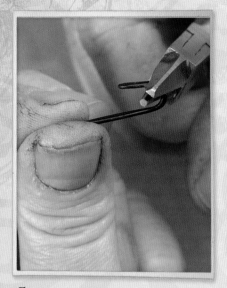

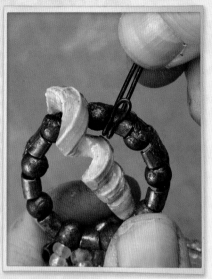

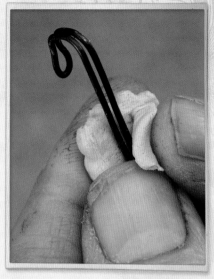

5. Bend the hammered wire into a hook, using round-nose pliers.

6. Check that the hook fits securely onto the found-object focal piece and that it isn't too tight.

7. Make a second hooked wire piece. Hold the wire hook up against the back of the lion's paw to make sure the flared ends of the wire do not extend out past the sides of the paw. (Adjust them with the pliers, if necessary.) Attach the wire hook onto the back of the lion's paw with some freshly mixed clay.

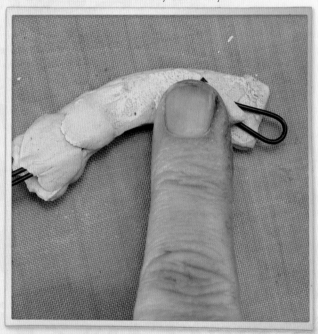

8. Attach a second hook to the other clay paw. Cut a 2" (5cm) piece of wire. Create a flared U shape with the pliers.

9. Attach the flared U shape to the other end of the paw element so that it extends out far enough to attach the necklace chain to it with a jump ring. Apply fresh clay and blend in all along the back and onto the sides.

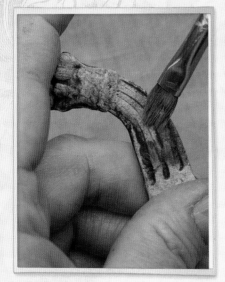

10. Repeat for the other end of the other paw. Begin applying thin washes of watered-down acrylic paint to the two clay pieces.

11. Apply a layer of Espresso alcohol ink and pewter metallic powder. You can mix small amounts of this at a time on your craft sheet.

12. Continue building up layers, then coat with acrylic varnish.

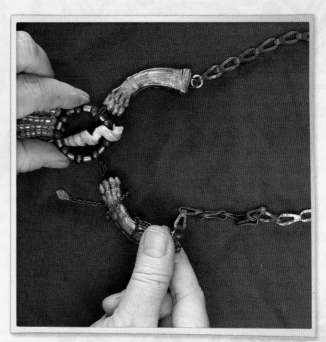

13. Cut some chain to the desired length. Attach each end to a lion's paw, using a jump ring and a couple pairs of pliers.

14. To close the necklace, both lion's paws will connect to the found-object focal piece.

For the May Queen
Necklace

Where'er I roam, whatever realms to see,
My heart untravelled, fondly turns to thee;
Still to my brother turns, with ceaseless pain,
And drags at each remove a lengthening chain.

—Oliver Goldsmith, The Traveler

I enjoy making my own chain when I can't find a premade one with just the right personality. When you create your own links, it opens up many possibilities. I often start by making a mold from what will be the piece's focal point and go from there. The wire you add can be in simple configurations or quite complex combinations of designs made on a jig, and an unlimited array of clay beaded elements with any type of finish imaginable.

This project is very simple and is really just the start of what can be done with these techniques. One thing I love about this is it is much faster to make than solid chain and infinitely more interesting!

Materials

silicone molding putty

unmixed epoxy clay

18-gauge steel wire

wire cutters

chain-nose pliers

steel bench block

hammer

craft knife

acrylic paints: your choice

paintbrush

acrylic varnish

jump rings

reclaimed chain, including clasp

beads and bead supplies (optional)

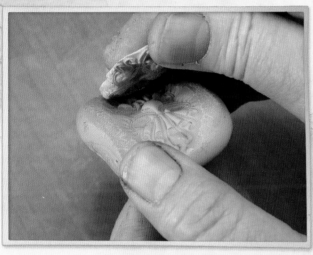

1. Begin by creating a mold for your links. Since several (eight to ten) links will need to be made to complete the necklace, you might want to create a few identical molds to speed up the production process. For this project, my links were about ¾" x 1½" (2cm x 4cm). Once you have a mold (or several), begin pressing mixed and uncured clay into the mold(s) and let cure.

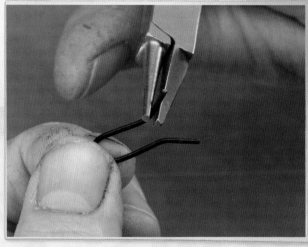

2. Cut two pieces of 18-gauge wire, each 1½" (4cm) long. Bend each wire piece into an elongated U shape. Flare out the ends slightly. Then place the wire on a steel bench block or anvil and hammer to flatten it.

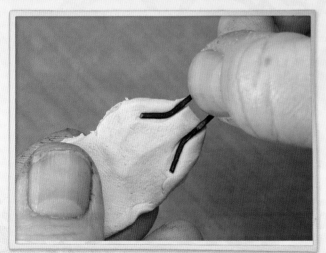

3. Apply a thin layer (about ⅟₁₆" [2mm] thick) of uncured clay to the back of each link. Then press one piece of bent wire into the clay on each end of the link. Allow the clay to cure. Repeat this for half of the remaining cured links.

4. Put one cured clay piece (one without wire) back to back with one piece that has wire. Press mixed and uncured clay into the gap between the two pieces. Clean up any excess clay with a craft knife. Repeat for the remaining links.

5. Using the mold you used to create the links (you may need to turn it inside out), apply texture to the uncured clay along the sides of each link. Allow all the uncured clay to cure.

6. Paint the links with acrylic paint. You can get a nice color variation by applying one shade of paint and wiping it off to reveal the raised areas. Then paint over just the raised areas with a different shade. Allow the paint to dry. Apply several layers of matte acrylic varnish, allowing each coat dry between applications.

7. Connect your finished links using jump rings.

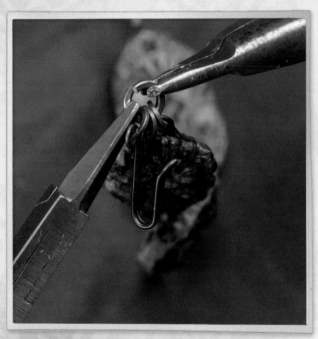

8. Add your chosen clasp with jump rings as well.

9. Attach beaded elements such as small tassels or attach charms and/or small found objects to the jump rings, as desired.

Peep Show
Kerin Gale

When I was visiting my daughter, Christine, I nearly fell off my chair when I noticed the awesome antique slides that she had placed in the window. (Well maybe it was the combination of that and the wine we were drinking.) In any case I really had to keep my composure when she told me she had been saving them for me! I knew immediately that I would somehow use at least one of these in a project for this book. On the spot I promised her a copy along with whatever I made so I hope you like this Chris!

Peep shows have been around for centuries in one form or another but perhaps this is the only one starring Miss Peep in her very first show. It was very simple to make a holder for the slide that would fit on the found (and headless) figure but one that I'd have a hard time figuring out how to make with any other material than epoxy clay.

I used distressed silver leaf on corrugated cardboard (who knew!) at the back of the stage and transparencies of the slide image in the side windows. By the way the cabinet cost under five dollars at a thrift store, and the heavy red velvet drapes were purchased at a garage sale. (They started out much larger though!)

Charm School
Nameplate Charm

Carve your name on hearts, not on marble.
—Charles Spurgeon

Popular names come and go and if we were making these back in Victorian times, some ladies' names we'd likely see would include Winnifred, Selina, Theodosia, Genevieve and Hannah. For the gents we might see Ambrose, Horatio, Meriwether, Jasper, Obediah and Eldon. The odds of knowing anyone with these names today aren't so likely. Unusual names still exist today, but anyone can be personalized with

these nameplate charms. These could also be used for organizing cabinets (think of making these into handles that also name the contents) or as gift tags. I wonder if having dyslexia helped me to think of "reverse casting" the resin and essentially building this backwards. I love that the front is all clear resin and the frame is just painted on.

Materials

vintage convention badge (or frame-like object with a flat surface)

silicone molding putty

clear liquid resin (ICE)

mixing containers and stir stick

word processing software, computer and printer

photo-editing software to make patterned background for name, etc. (optional)

scissors

acrylic gloss medium

paintbrushes

18-gauge steel wire

wire cutters

steel bench block or anvil

hammer

unmixed epoxy clay

mold to provide texture

acrylic paint: copper (Modern Options)

acrylic matte varnish

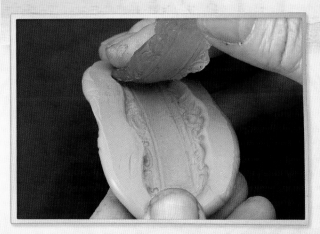

1. Create a mold from a vintage convention badge. Mix liquid resin following the manufacturer's instructions. Pour it into the mold and allow it to harden. Then remove the hardened resin from the mold.

2. Prepare the words you'll place in the flat area of the charm. You can create the words using word processing or photo-editing software. Be sure to size the words to fit on the charm. Print them and cut them out.

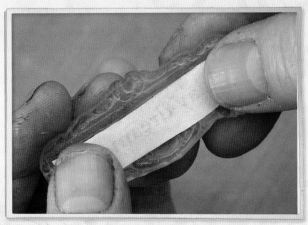

3. Apply a thin layer of gloss medium to the back side of the resin casting. (You know you have the right amount of medium when the paintbrush glides over the resin surface with no drag.) Then press the printed words facedown into the gloss medium (so that the words are facing out when viewing the front of the resin casting).

4. Apply a thin layer of gloss medium to the back of the casting, over the paper. This will protect the word from any discoloration the clay may cause when added.

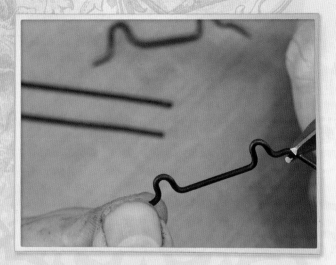

5. Cut two 3" (8cm) pieces of 18-gauge wire and bend each into a U shape, containing two smaller U shapes, as shown.

6. Place each wire on a bench block or anvil and hammer the wire to flatten.

7. Attach the two pieces of wire to the back of the resin charm (securing with tape, if necessary), one at the top and one at the bottom, all loops facing out. Place them so that the wire does not sit on the paper word (and show through to the other side). Mix up a small amount of clay to hold the wires in place. Add a layer of clay to the entire back side of the resin casting. Allow the clay to cure. Then apply a little more clay, if needed, so that the back is flat. Allow it to cure.

8. Prepare a texture mold. Add another thin layer of clay to the back of the charm. Apply the texture mold to the back, bringing it around toward the front to round off the edges. Allow to cure.

Inspired Tip

eBay is a great resource for finding obscure pieces from which to make molds. Some of the best for nameplate charms are vintage fraternal organization and political name tags. If you go to ebay under # Home > # Buy > # Collectibles > # Historical Memorabilia > # Fraternal Organizations > you'll likely find many suitable items that can be used for this project. The best ones will have a flat or domed area, which is where you'll add the name. If it has a dimensional design in this area, the name won't be as easy to read.

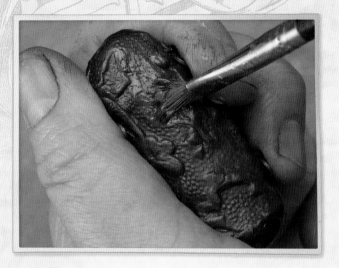

9. Paint around the frame on the front and the entire back with acrylic paint. (I like using metallics.) Seal with matte varnish, if desired.

10. Apply a thin layer of gloss varnish to the front of the charm over the words. This will help the word show up a bit better because it changes the surface from a matte finish, which is more opaque, to a gloss finish, which is more transparent.

From the Gallery

Dryad

Rebecca Schumacher

One of a kind bas-relief on board in oak frame, sculpted completely with Aves Apoxie Sculpt and painted with acrylics.

48" x 20"

Time Passing
Altered Pocket Watch

"The time is gone, the song is over, thought I'd something more to say"
—David Gilmour/Nick Mason/Roger Waters/Richard Wright
from "Time" Performed by Pink Floyd

Our collective fascination with time—especially objective time—is the inspiration for this piece. It seems that our perception of the rate of time passing is more significant to our experience than actually measuring time accurately. Since time seems to go by so much faster when we are engaged in an experience, those are the moments that make up the memories we carry with us. Does anyone have fond memories of waiting in line or caught in traffic? Doubtful those will be the things remembered at life's end.

For your consideration here is a timepiece containing the crystallization of memories from the sands of time—fragments of memories that we carry with us wherever we go. Placing clay over the pocket watch creates a slightly irregular shape and is reminiscent of bending time. Pressing the wire screen into the clay creates a hazy boundary between the two materials like the gray area between this world and the next.

Materials

metal screening, small piece

small dish

clear glass pebbles, small

tin snips

empty pocket watch case

nonstick craft sheet

unmixed epoxy clay (Apoxie Sculpt, black)

charms, keys, or other found object(s) (optional)

acrylic paint: iron (Modern Options)

rusting solution (Modern Options)

acrylic matte varnish

paintbrushes

linen thread and beads for necklace

clasp

Introducing Apoxie Sculpt

Aves Studios makes many formulas of clays. Until now, we've been using the fixit Sculpt formula, which is only available in one color. There may be times when you want the clay itself to have a certain color. Since we need a dark color inside the watch, this is a great time to use the Apoxie Sculpt formula, which comes in many colors including black and brown. Either one will work for this project.

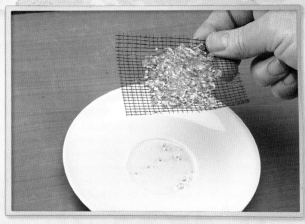

1. Place a piece of screen over a dish and pour the glass pebbles onto the screen. Shake the screen to sift out the pebbles that are too small to be held by the screen. Remove these pebbles. Set aside the pebbles that won't fit through the screen.

2. Cut the screen into a circle big enough to cover the opening in the watch but not so large that it protrudes beyond the outer edge of the watch. Begin by cutting less to start with so the screen doesn't start out too small.

3. Cover the sides and back of the watch with a thin layer of mixed and uncured clay. You can leave some bumpy texture, though, because the piece is meant to look rustic.

4. Cover the entire inside of the watch with a thin layer of clay as well.

5. Place a ring of uncured clay around the perimeter of the watch face. Blend it in with the clay on the sides and inside. Allow all the clay (back and inside) to cure.

6. Pour the glass pebbles (from step 1) into the watch case until it is about two-thirds full. Also add any charms, skeleton keys or other tiny found objects, if desired.

7. Place the round piece of screen on top of the watch to cover the empty face. Add some newly mixed clay to the edges of the screen and blend it in with the clay around the perimeter to secure. Allow the clay to cure.

8. Paint the clay with iron paint and rust activator following the manufacturer's instructions. Allow the paint to dry. Seal with a matte varnish.

9. Determine how long you'd like the necklace to be and cut two or more pieces of linen thread that long plus 4" (10cm). Fold the linen thread strands in half and attach them to the necklace by looping the linen thread around the loop on top of the watch. Attach beads, if desired, and add a clasp.

Buster Bee
Christine Lehto
23"W x 16"H x 15"D

Sea Pea Pod
Pendant

Live in the sunshine, swim the sea, drink the wild air . . .
— Ralph Waldo Emerson

Two years ago we were living in Washington and due to several significant events happening, we both realized that we weren't living where we wanted to and we wanted to spend more time creating and sharing art. So, in the middle of a recession, we decided to "run away" to the southern coast of Oregon to be near the ocean and live a different kind of life.

We are much happier today than we were, even with the bumps in the road we encountered. One of the huge blessings is all the natural beauty that surrounds us. The sea is definitely a muse to us both

and the Sea Pea Pod was heavily inspired by our surroundings. This year was an especially good harvest of sea pods, and this pendant is just bursting with plump little shells. If you look closely, you can see the tiny bubbles from when they are washed ashore.

One exciting use of epoxy clay is as an armature under polymer clay. Epoxy clay is a lot stronger than polymer, and I selected this project to show how easily the two can be combined and baked together right in the oven.

Materials

- silicone molding putty or tinfoil
- nonstick craft sheet
- unmixed epoxy clay (Fixit Sculpt)
- green and translucent polymer clay
- clay roller and/or pasta machine used for polymer
- silicone clay shaper tool (optional)
- solvent ink pad

- rubber stamp alphabet (optional)
- polyester fiberfill, small amount
- oven to bake the polymer clay
- acrylic paint: dark green
- alcohol ink: Sage Green (Adirondak)
- paintbrushes
- masking tape
- drill or pin vise and $1/16$" (2mm) drill bit

- micro bolts, 2
- craft glue
- small seashells
- liquid resin, mixing cup and stir stick (ICE Resin)
- gloss medium (Diamond Glaze)
- glass micro beads
- wire for hanging (preferably reclaimed and wonderfully aged)
- glass leaves on wire (or other glass beads)
- jewelry findings (including a clasp) of your choice for the necklace

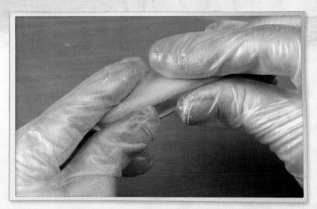

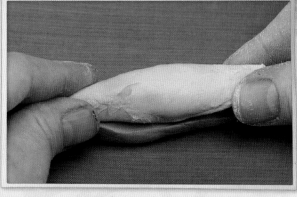

1. Create a nonstick support by molding silicone compound into a pod shape. (Alternatively, you could use tinfoil.) Place down on a nonstick craft sheet until fully cured.

2. Shape mixed, uncured clay into a pea pod form. The pod should be thinly walled and open in the center (to hold the shell "peas"). When it's sculpted, place the pod facedown on top of the silicone or foil form, and allow the clay to cure.

3. Prepare the polymer clay: Mix two parts green clay to one part translucent clay. Roll the clay flat and paper thin.

4. Wrap the polymer clay sheet around the epoxy clay pod. Smooth and blend the edges with your fingers and/or a silicone clay shaper tool.

  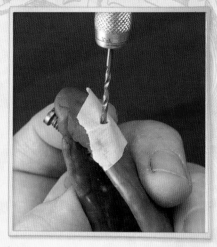

5. Set out letter stamps to spell the word of your choice. Flip the pod on its side, press each letter onto an ink pad and then into the polymer clay.

6. Bake the pod according to the polymer clay manufacturer's instructions, supported on small amount of fiberfill. Remove from the oven and allow to cool. Load a liberal amount of dark green acrylic paint onto your paintbrush. Squirt a generous puddle of Sage Green alcohol ink onto a nonstick craft sheet. Quickly mix the paint on the brush into the puddle of ink and immediately apply to the pod. If the mixture starts to get gummy, rinse the brush and repeat as needed to cover the interior and exterior of the pod.

7. Decide how you want the pod pendant to hang (vertically or horizontally) and mark where the bolts will go. Make sure to select a spot where the clay is thin enough so that the length of the bolts will go into the interior of the pod. Then apply a small piece of masking tape where you will drill the hole (to help keep the clay from chipping). Slowly and carefully drill the holes with either a hand drill or a pin vise with a ¹⁄₁₆" (2mm) drill bit. Place the bolts into the holes with enough of the bolt on the outside to wrap the wire around. Apply some craft glue to fill in any gaps around the bolt.

8. Using craft glue, secure the seashells to the inside of the pod. Allow the glue to dry thoroughly.

9. Mix the liquid resin according to the manufacturer's instructions. Carefully pour a small amount of resin into the pod, just enough to go about halfway up the shells. Check for any large air bubbles. Pour the remaining resin into the pod. Do this very slowly so that you don't overfill the pod. Again check for any large air bubbles and remove them with a toothpick (or by passing a flame or your warm breath over the surface). I intentionally left some small air bubbles to enhance the "sea" theme of the piece. Rest the pod back on the fiberfill making sure it is level and allow the resin to fully cure.

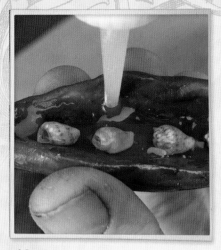  

10. Apply a small amount of gloss medium around the edge of the resin where it meets the wall of the pod.

11. Sprinkle glass micro beads in the gloss medium. Then sparingly apply more gloss medium over the top of the micro beads to hold them in place. Allow the medium to dry.

12. Wrap the glass leaves with wire and attach to the bolts with wire, allowing some space to then attach the necklace. Finish by attaching some sort of necklace (beads or a chain) to the wires.

From the Gallery

Victorian Journal
Brenda Gebhart

Persephone
Tassel

Art! Who comprehends her? With whom can one consult concerning this great goddess?
—Ludwig van Beethoven

One day last year my mom suddenly became ill and was admitted to the hospital. I was getting over the flu but mustered up some energy to head down to Sacramento where my mom was.

I knew I needed to stop somewhere to take a walk break and keep myself alert. I remembered a group of antique stores just north of Redding, so I set the course on the GPS, flipped on the cruise control and crawled into the backseat for a little nap. When I arrived at the antique stores, I felt rested and ready to explore the nooks and crannies. When I first saw the floor lamp with the three goddesses around the bottom, I remember thinking it was a bit spendy, but I knew it would be versatile for so many things.

I repeated the same thing to Charley when he looked at the bill. Justification for the sake of art reigns supreme!

So far the mold made from one of the goddesses has been made into this tassel—a mechanical mermaid that swishes her tail and dances when the handle is turned. It was an element in a fun collaborative project called "Disintegration" on Seth Apter's Altered Page blog (a great place to visit!).

When making a mold of a larger piece such as this, it is especially helpful to use the slow-curing silicone mold material from Silpak. It would be very tricky to try to make a large mold with most of the other formulas I've used.

Materials

object to mold a
torso from

silicone molding
putty

unmixed epoxy clay

19-gauge wire

wire cutters

tassel elements
(beaded strands,
assorted chain,
fibers, found
objects, charms)

masking tape

acrylic paints:
your choice

paintbrushes

nonstick craft
sheet

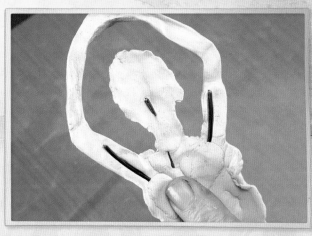

1. Make a press mold of a goddess figure. The figure I had didn't
have a back; I only had the front so I made two castings so
the front and back of the tassel will look the same. If you use
a three-dimensional mold the front and back can be different,
but cast the two sides separately. Mix up enough epoxy clay to
fill your molds and cast your figure. Allow to cure.

2. Reinforce any thin areas of your casting by embedding
lengths of wire into some freshly mixed clay. Allow to cure.

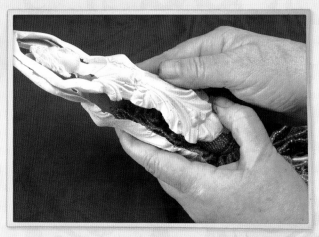

3. Gather strands of beads and various chains together. Cut a
12" (31cm) length of 19-gauge wire and create an elongated
U shape. Lay the strands over the loop in the wire, and
adjust the strands so that the lengths are balanced on either
side of the wire. Gently twist the wire just enough to hold
the strands firmly together without breaking any of the glass
beads or other fragile elements.

4. Fold up the remaining wire and sandwich the tassel between
the two halves of the figure. Press them together to make
sure the tassel fits. Temporarily tape the wires in place on the
inside of one of the castings, using masking tape. Then, apply
fresh clay to secure the wires to the casting. The tape will
hold the wires in place while the clay cures.

5. Apply the second casting and combine the two pieces with freshly mixed clay to adhere together. Blend the fresh clay into the cured clay all along the edges and allow to fully cure. If the gap is too wide, place some masking or duct tape across the gap before adding the clay.

6. Apply paint colors of your choice in thin washes (paint mixed with water). Here, I used green and brown mixed together with water on the craft sheet and then applied to the goddess figure.

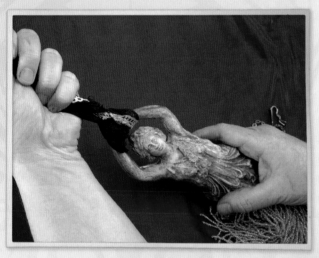

7. Attach fibers or chain to the top of the figure for a hanger.

Inspired Tip

If the figure of your torso doesn't have a natural place to hang the tassel such as the overhead clasped hands of this goddess, use a much longer piece of wire to bind the tassel strands together and bring the wire up through the top of your castings to create a hanger. You can embellish the wire hanger by wrapping with fibers, adding more beads and/or chains.

8. Drape the goddess with additional chain and bead strands.

Marguarite Oiseau

Chris Chomick

Sculpted with Magic
Sculpt epoxy clay
over Styrofoam and
braided armature
wire. Head, arms and
bird legs are hand
painted with acryl-
ics and varnished.
Bird legs are cast
pewter and mount-
ed to the base with
brass tubes.

$15\frac{1}{2}$"H x 6"W x 9"D

photo by Peter Meder

Memento Mori
Cross

Do you realize that everyone you know someday will die?
And instead of saying all of your goodbyes
Let them know you realize that life goes fast
It's hard to make the good things last.
—Wayne Coyne, "Do You Realize?"
Performed by the Flaming Lips

Memento mori is a Latin phrase that reminds us of our mortality. It means "Remember, you must die." Using antique casket hardware to make a cross seemed an appropriate use of materials to convey a sense of time passing, the power of our beliefs and the mortality we all must face. This project is so easy and can be adapted to solve many challenges in combining found objects. Epoxy clay is the perfect "fill in" to both adhere pieces that may not exactly fit together and to add strength to the piece.

This is probably the thing I love most about epoxy clay: With a bit of determination, I can figure out how to make just about any piece of jewelry or found object assemblage even if the parts don't fit together exactly. How exciting to have this kind of freedom and infinite possibilities!

Materials

casket hardware
thumbscrews, 2

casket hardware
faceplate

permanent marker,
fine point

rotary tool with
cutting blade, or
saw to cut metal

unmixed epoxy clay

drill and $^1/_{16}$" (2mm)
drill bit

swatch of red velvet

craft glue

micro scissors (or
fingernail scissors)

thread and needle

tatted lace

faceted crystal bead

jewelry findings or
wire to make handmade
hooks

aged wire

wire cutters

jewelry pliers

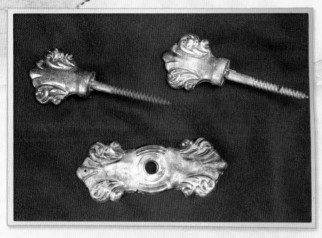

1. For this project, you will need three pieces of antique casket hardware (or similar objects): two thumbscrews and a faceplate. The faceplate will be set horizontally and the thumbnail screws vertically (one up and one down).

2. Place the hardware facedown in a cross shape (as described in step 1). Determine how long the thumbscrews should be; you want to remove any parts that extend beyond the center of the faceplate. Using a fine-point marker, mark where to cut and with a jewelry saw or cutting wheel on the rotary tool, remove the unwanted lengths of the screws.

3. Apply mixed uncured clay to the back of the faceplate. Press the two thumbscrews into the clay. Add more clay as needed to secure. Allow the clay to cure.

4. Mark the placement of the hole for the jump rings in the center of each end of the faceplate, near the edge.

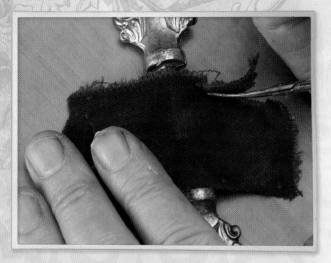

5. Drill the holes in the faceplace using a drill and ¹⁄₁₆" (2mm) bit. Cut a piece of thick fabric—such as the vintage velvet—slightly larger than the back of the faceplate. Glue it into place using a strong craft adhesive (like Tacky Glue) and allow the glue to dry. Trim the excess fabric around the edges of the faceplate using sharp micro scissors.

6. Using the strong adhesive, glue a small piece of tattered lace (if the edges aren't frayed tear them by hand to give a ragged appearance) to the front, middle of the cross. Then cut out a small red heart from the thick fabric. Glue that on top of the lace.

7. Glue the top of a faceted crystal bead to a piece of the red velvet. Sew this onto the bottom of the velvet heart. Add additional embellishments, such as the antique silver button I used, as desired.

8. Make a mixed-media necklace to complement the cross. I used wire-wrapped velvet with tattered lace and glass buttons, silver filigree beads, grey glass beads, smoky quartz beads, round bloodstone beads, small pieces of French netted lace and vintage rhinestone circles. I also added old silver-colored washers that I collaged with vintage papers and embellished with silver and grey beads.

Inspired Tip

If you have pieces of fabric and lace that appear too new for an antique piece, you can fake a vintage look. Simply dip pieces in a cup of brewed tea and allow to dry.

Merrily We Roll Along
Judy Anderson

Constructed from a smoked oyster can, wooden wheels, brass candleholder, plastic Christmas ornament, plastic bubble blower stem and miscellaneous mechanical parts, Merrily We Roll Along is a social comment on life. One minute we are rolling along and everything is just fine and in an instant life changes, as depicted by the alternate side of the piece and its ominous figurine with tacks in the tires. Epoxy clay was used in many intricate small areas to hold desperate objects. Aves Apoxie Clay was placed on the back of the bolts where tightening a small nut would not have been possible.

Fly Like a Bird
Marlaine Verhelst

The piece is about believing in yourself. Even if everyone says that you are nuts (to think you can fly with wings this small), just go for it. Resin clay is strong and makes it possible to create thin legs and other fine body parts.

12" x 10" x 10"

57

Secrets of My Heart
Locket

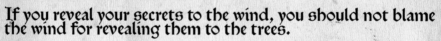

If you reveal your secrets to the wind, you should not blame the wind for revealing them to the trees.

—Kahlil Gibran

Secret compartments, hidden passageways, trick locks and configuration puzzles with interlocking pieces—I love them all.

I was so tickled when, in the middle of the night, the answer came to me on how to make this, it was all I could do to not go out to the studio and begin working on it right away. It was so fun to see that my editor was not quite sure how to open it during the photo shoot even though she knew the basic idea of how it worked.

Being able to use precision shapes made of chipboard or cardstock opens so many possibilities for using epoxy clay to create a multitude of hidden compartments and the like. This project uses an embedded hinge to open the locket in an unusual way, thereby making it a bit tricky or "secret" to open. If I added a backplate with magnets and matching magnets on the back, this locket wouldn't open at all unless it was pulled off from the back and even then it would take a little bit of exploring to see how to open it.

Try this for yourself and see what deviously creative ideas you'll get from using hidden hinges and such to make your own hiding places.

Materials

chipboard

heart punch or paper pattern

scissors

unmixed epoxy clay

texture mold, rubber stamp or other texturing tools

cardstock

ruler

masking tape

small hinge

19-gauge wire

round-nose pliers

drill and $^1/_{16}$" (2mm) drill bit

acrylic paints: light brown, burgundy, dark brown

paintbrush

paper towel

alcohol ink: Cranberry (Adirondak)

black tatted lace (or white lace stained with black ink)

jewelry glue

ribbon or chain and clasp of your choice

micro bolt

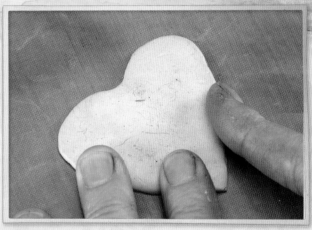

1. Cut or punch two identical heart shapes (with about a 2" [5cm] diameter) from chipboard.

2. Place a thin layer of mixed, uncured clay over one chipboard heart. (Set aside the other one for now.) Smooth the edges with a bit of water. Allow the clay to cure.

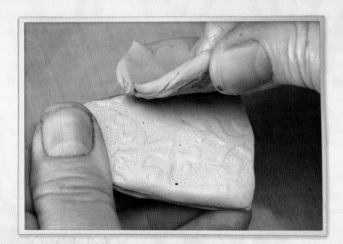

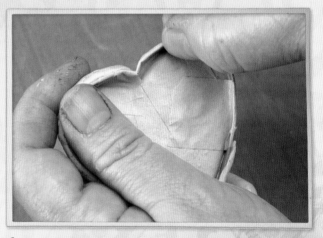

3. Add another thin layer of mixed, uncured clay over the cured clay. Use a texture mold (or rubber stamp or any other texturing tool) to add texture to the uncured clay. This will be the back of the locket.

4. Cut a strip of cardstock about ¼" (6mm) wide and 10" (25cm) long. Using masking tape, attach the strip to the edges of the clay heart (with the textured side on the back) to form the sides of what will look like a heart box. Trim the excess from the strip as necessary.

59

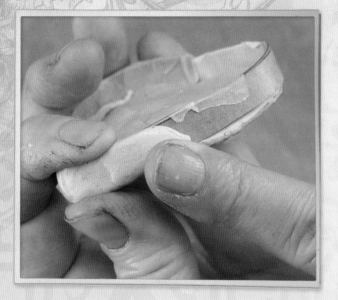

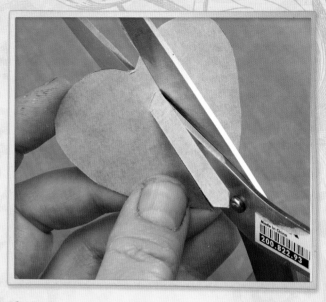

5. Apply a thin layer of mixed, uncured clay over the chipboard strip and down into the heart to secure the two together and to cover up the masking tape. Smooth the clay with a little water at the seams. Set this heart aside and allow the clay to cure.

6. Cut out a 5/16" (8mm) strip from middle of the second chipboard heart (running from the point straight up to the V).

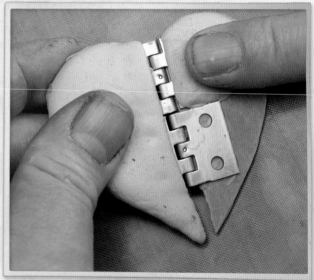

7. Apply mixed, uncured clay to one side of each half of the heart. Smooth the edges with a bit of water. Allow the clay to cure.

8. Turn both halves over and position them together with the small hinge running between them. The rounded part of the hinge should be facing away from you and the flat side facing up. Attach the hinge to each half of the heart with mixed, uncured clay, blending the clay around the sides with a little water as needed.

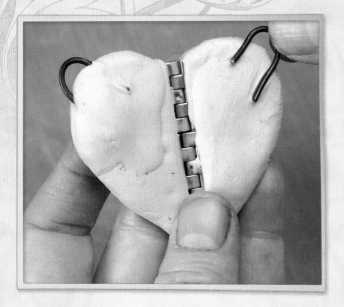

9. Bend two 2" (5cm) pieces of wire into simple U shapes, using round-nose pliers. Attach each wire piece to the top of each half of the hinged heart. Embed the wire in the uncured clay. Allow the clay to cure.

10. Either free-hand or using a mold, sculpt a small, flat hand about 1" (3cm) long. Create a small hole in the middle of the hand. Also mark a corresponding hole in the center of the heart box where you wish to secure the hand, using the hand as a guide. Drill the hole in the cured box, using a power or hand drill and a ¹⁄₁₆" (2mm) bit.

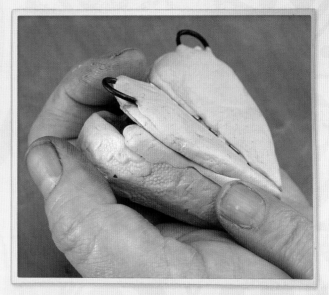

11. Paint the hand with light brown acrylic paint and allow it to dry. Then apply watered-down dark brown acrylic paint. Wipe away some of the excess paint, using a paper towel, to give the hand an aged appearance. Allow the paint to dry thoroughly and the clay hand to fully cure.

12. Place the hinged heart on top of the heart box. Attach one half of the hinged heart to the box. Here, I have secured the left half, so that the box will open by raising the right half which was left unattached. Start by adding mixed, uncured clay to the the straight edge and then around the curve. Add enough clay to make the piece secure and smooth the seams.

13. Paint the entire locket with burgundy acrylic paint mixed with Cranberry alcohol ink.

14. Brush on watered-down, dark brown acrylic paint, and then wipe some of the paint off with a paper towel, leaving an aged appearance. Allow the paint to dry thoroughly.

15. Cut four sections of black tatted lace—three for the points on the heart and a smaller one for on top of the hand. Attach the lace using jewelry glue. Then attach the hand to the heart using a micro bolt.

16. Add ribbon, a strip of velvet, chain or beaded clasp to the loops on the locket, as desired.

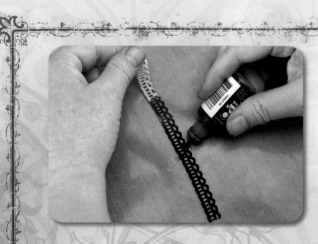

Inspired Tip

Sometimes it is difficult to find black tatted lace. If that is the case, dye white tatted lace with black alcohol ink.

From the Gallery

Cyclopian Brush Boy
Michael deMeng

"This little dude stands about 12" tall and combines Apoxy clay with a broken doll, an angel statuette, a T-Rex toy and a brush."

Reluctant Prince
Nancy Perennec

"His body is sculpted entirely by hand in Apoxie Sculpt over a wire armature. His crown, made from Apoxie with embellishments can be removed from his head. He wears velveteen pants, a hand-stitched and beaded cod piece, a hand-pleated shirt and jeweled origami-style boots of gold."
17" tall

Vintage Gentleman
Encased Portrait

A tramp, a gentleman, a poet, a dreamer, a lonely fellow, always hopeful of romance and adventure.

—Charlie Chaplin

One of the reasons we rearranged our life and moved to another state is to be able to share some of our art discoveries with other artists. Teaching is such a rewarding experience. This technique is one we have taught live and online, and it's a very fun process with unlimited possibilities. Essentially, we'll be making a sandwich for an image between resin and clay.

For this Vintage Gent we'll also incorporate rivets. Being able to rivet onto the cured epoxy clay is yet another testament to how strong this material is. By pouring resin into a mold with a very shallow dimensional design we create what I call textured resin—a piece that has a visible design, yet still shows off an image placed beneath

it. Another great effect we use is taking a gloss medium and by putting that on just a portion of cured resin, it turns transparent rather than opaque. When seen in person, the play of light on the surface of the image underneath is amazing. Finally, I reveal here one of my favorite recipes to mimic old tooled leather on the back and also show you how to do Charley's design for the unique bale which is riveted in place.

I think you'll really enjoy making this project since it has so many techniques I've developed that are new for you to try. And hopefully, this will be just the beginning as you play around with these ideas on other pieces, too!

Materials

liquid resin, mixing cup and stir stick

amber resin colorant (optional)

silicone mold of an antique daguerreotype or a decorative rectangular element, to look similar

photocopy of a vintage portrait image that will fit your premade mold

small paintbrush

scissors

gloss medium (Diamond Glaze)

unmixed epoxy clay

binder clips

clay shaper (optional)

craft knife

paper towels or disposable wipes

19-gauge steel wire

round-nose pliers

ballpeen hammer

steel bench block or anvil

alcohol ink: Espresso (Adirondack)

palette or disposable surface

acrylic paint: burnt umber

medium or fine sandpaper

12-gauge copper wire nails (at least ¾" [19mm] long), 4

matte medium

weathering powder: Dirty Brown (Doc O'Brien's)

pencil

Dremel tool or drill with ⁵⁄₆₄" (2mm) drill bit

small washers that fit your 12-gauge nails snugly, 10

metal spacer beads with hole that fit your 12-gauge nails snugly, 10

wire cutters

metal file

beading wire

small black beads

crimp tubes, 2

crimping pliers

1. Mix the liquid resin according to the manufacturer's instructions, adding a pin-prick amount of resin colorant to tint the resin very slightly. Pour into the mold and allow to cure fully. Pop the cured resin from the mold.

2. Use the resin as a guide over your vintage image to determine what portion of the image you will use. Apply gloss medium to the backside of the resin piece using a paintbrush. You want an even coating—not too thick and not too runny. Carefully position the image against the side of the resin with the gloss medium. Gently burnish the image against the resin to remove any bubbles and to ensure good adhesion. Set aside to dry.

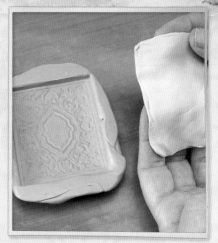

3. Prepare a thin piece of mixed clay for the mold.

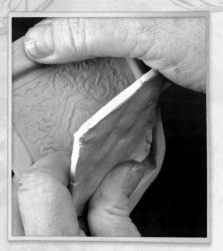

4. Using your fingers, work the clay into the mold, pressing gently and evenly to ensure you get the clay to all of the edges and against the entire textured part of the mold.

5. When the clay has cured, remove it from the mold. File down any high areas from the edges using drywall screen. To do this, first place a disposable wipe on the table, then set the drywall screen on top of the wipe. Drag the cured clay edges over the screen and the dust will be captured in the wipe.

6. Place the cured clay piece on the back of the resin piece so that both textured surfaces are facing out and the photo is between the two. Clip with binder clips. Then, make a snake of mixed clay (about the size of four peas) and press the clay into the gaps along the sides, and between the front and back pieces. Smooth the clay with a drop of water on your finger. (Rubbing your finger back and forth really helps to get the clay down into the gaps. You can also use the tip of a clay shaper dipped in water to get into the areas where your finger can't reach.)

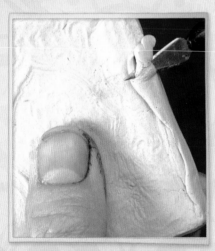

7. Remove the binder clips and work on any areas that still need clay. Carefully cut away any clay that goes over either side using a craft knife at an angle. Wipe away any excess clay from the front or back with a disposable wipe. Allow the piece to cure.

8. Cut two pieces of 19-gauge steel wire that are about 2" (5cm) long. On one end, make a small loop using round-nose pliers. On the other end, make a larger loop, as shown. Repeat for the second piece of wire.

9. Flatten the two wire shapes a bit using a hammer on a steel anvil or bench block.

10. Get a bit of water on the small paintbrush and dip it into a drop of Espresso alcohol ink. Working quickly, paint on the ink starting from the clay frame and moving around into just the edges of the resin front. Then load some burnt umber acrylic paint on the paintbrush. Put a generous puddle of Espresso alcohol ink onto a palette. Mix the paint and the ink together. Quickly apply as much as you can over the surface of the back of the piece. Let the mixture dry and then add a second coat. Gently sand the raised texture. Dip a brush in a puddle of matte medium and then into the Doc O'Brien's powder and tap, tap, tap to lightly mix. It should look fairly dry. Tap onto the surface of the painted piece. Lightly rub with a paper towel or disposable wipe to remove some of the paint and powder. Repeat for a well-worn look. Allow everything to dry and the clay to cure thoroughly.

Using a pencil, mark a spot in each corner where the holes for the rivets will go. Then drill the holes using a drill and ⁵⁄₆₄" (2mm) drill bit.

11. Insert one copper wire nail through a spacer, a washer and then through the front of the clay piece.

12. Flip the piece over and place a washer and spacer on each wire. At the top, place the two hammered-wire hangers created in steps 8 and 9 first and then the washers/spacers. (The washers and spacers should be a snug fit with little room for play around the wire.) Using heavy wire cutters, cut the excess wire, leaving just a fraction of wire above each spacer or hanger. File the wires as flat as possible to remove the bevels left from the cutters.

Working on an anvil or steel bench block, use a ball-peen hammer to tap around the perimter of each wire, to splay the wire out and create a rivet. This will secure the pieces in place.

13. Create a hanger for the piece using stringing wire, black beads and additional washers/spacers. Start with about 15" (38cm) of wire. String on a crimp bead and about 14 black beads. Thread the end of the wire through one of the hangers on the clay piece and back through the crimp bead and crimp to secure. Add a crimp cover, then thread on a washer and spacer and then about 10" (25cm) worth of black beads. Thread on another crimp bead, spacer, washer and 14 final black beads. Thread the strand through the other wire hanger, back through the crimp bead and pull taut before crimping. Cover with a second crimp cover and thread the excess wire through the strand of beads.

Nightwing
Evening Bag

**Strange things blow in through my window on the wings
of the night wind and I don't worry about my destiny.**

—Carl Sanburg

I almost always laugh when I think about the first time my friend
Jenny Dill saw this bag as a work-in-progress. She thought the raw
clay bird was so ugly. She thought I was crazy to think it should go in
an art book, though she didn't say anything at the time. When she
saw the finished bag, however, she absolutely loved it!

I want to reassure you that if you make an "ugly" bird,
it's nothing to fret over. Don't give up in frustration before it's
finished because there really is a kind of magic transformation
that takes place. I imagine this being the perfect bag to take out
for a night on the town.

Materials

lightweight tinfoil (not heavy-duty)

black or dark-colored silk fabric or reclaimed silk from shirt (for bag lining)

scissors

masking tape

unmixed epoxy clay

pliers

marking pen or pencil

hand drill with $\frac{1}{16}$" (2mm) drill bit

16-gauge steel rebar/tie wire

wire cutters

knitting needle or piece of tubing for winding spring hinge

vise (optional)

craft glue

black fabric for outside, such as velvet, embroidered velvet, embroidered rayon and net lace with beads

sewing needle

black thread

buttons for eyes

buttons and loops or other type of closure

1. Using a picture or drawing as a reference, sculpt a raven shape from tinfoil. This should be slightly smaller than your desired bag size. To sculpt curves and get a good shape, crumple smaller amounts of the foil to form the shape and then apply another larger sheet of foil over the entire piece to hold it in place. The size of this foil bird will be the inside dimensions of your evening bag so take that into account when you are trying to gauge size.

2. Cut a generous amount of silk to fit around the bird shape with at least 6" (15cm) extra to be gathered at the top, in the middle of the bird's back. Drape the silk around the bird and gather the excess fabric together. (Note: If you are using a fabric that has a right and wrong side, be sure to have the wrong side facing out.)

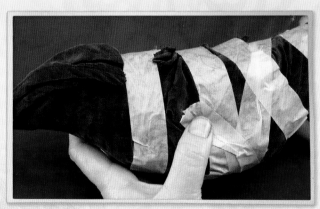

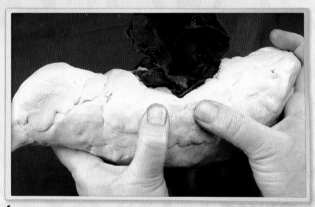

3. Tape the fabric together with masking tape to hold it around the foil form.

4. Cover the bird form with clay leaving an oval opening on the back of the bird. This will be the opening of the bag so plan accordingly (make sure it will be large enough to put your hand down into). Remove any masking tape necessary in order to pull the excess gathered silk out of the oval hole. (Note: The silk will bond with the clay and create an instant lining and will also keep the clay from sticking to the tinfoil bird form.)

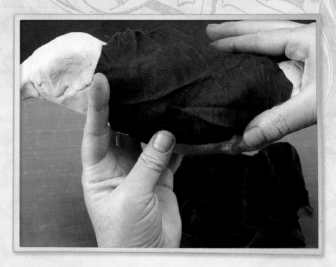

5. Place some extra bunched-up silk on your work surface. Set the bird upside down on the silk "nest" and allow the clay to cure fully. The nest will prevent any flat spots from forming while the clay cures.

6. Using the oval opening in the top of the bird as a reference, cut a large oval piece of silk at least 2" (5cm) larger than the opening on the bird.

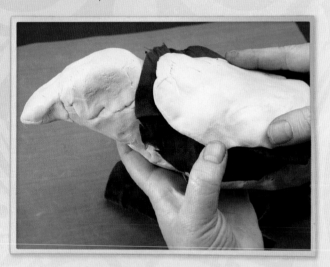

7. Sculpt an oval lid that overhangs about ½" (13mm) all around the opening on the top of the bird. Gently press it onto the bird so that it follows the curved contours of the bird's back. Place the oval piece of silk over the opening and place the clay oval on top of the silk. Allow to fully cure.

8. Set the lid aside. Open up the gathered silk and remove all the foil from inside the bird with a pair of pliers or your hands.

Inspired Tip

Other design ideas you might want to try:
- Add legs and claws so the bird stands on its own
- Scale it down and perhaps make a different kind of bird with colorful fibers, fabric remnants and feathers.
- Add a nest to the bottom that travels along with the bird.
- Cover the bird with mosaics.
- Add wings with secret stash pockets.

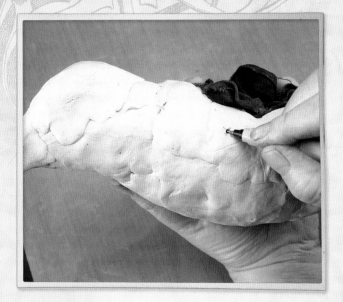

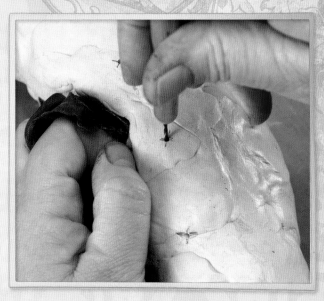

9. You're now going to drill two holes into the bird body; these will hold a hinge that will attach to the lid. Using the lid as a guide, determine where the two holes will go. Mark these spots with a marking pen or pencil, at least ½" (13mm) below the edge of the lid and about ½" (13mm) inward from each end of the lid. Also mark where you will drill the corresponding holes on the lid.

10. Holding the lining fabric out of the way (use masking tape to hold it if you need to), drill all the holes (on the bag and the lid) using a hand drill and a ¹⁄₁₆" (2mm) drill bit.

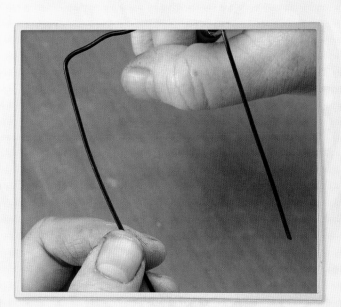

11. Cut one piece of wire three-and-a-half times longer than the width between the two holes on the bird's body. Bend the wire at right angles as shown, leaving the middle section of the wire the same length as the distance between the two holes.

12. Cut a second length of wire, about 3' (91cm) long. Leaving a 3" (8cm) tail from one end of the wire, begin wrapping the wire in a tight spiral around a large knitting needle or a wood dowel. (You may want to put the knitting needle or dowel in a vise to hold it while you wrap.) When the coil is ¼" (6mm) shorter than the distance between the two drilled holes, stop coiling and position the two tails of wire so they are parallel. This spring will be a hinge for the lid opening.

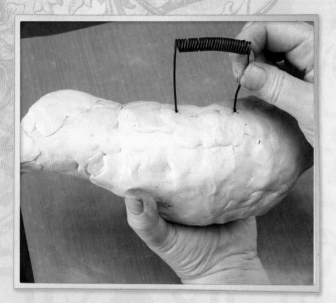

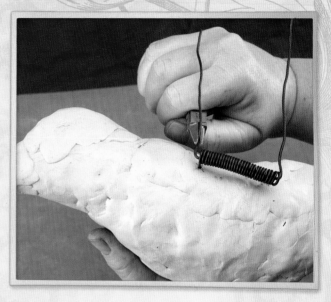

13. Pulling the fabric temporarily out of the way, insert the spring into the two holes on the bird that are for attaching the lid. The wires should go down all the way into the bird, and the spring should be flush with the surface of the bird.

14. Straighten out one of the right angles on the wire piece created in step 11 and run it through the outside hinge piece. Then bend the straightened end of the wire back up at a 90-degree angle.

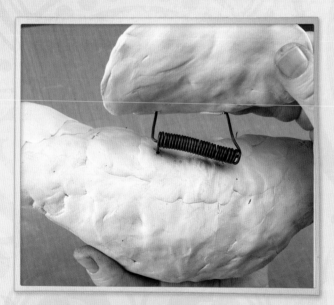

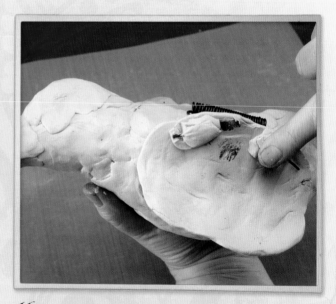

15. Insert the loose wire ends into the holes on the lid. Adjust the spring hinge if necessary.

16. Bend in the loose wires on the underside of the lid to hold the wire in place. Clip the excess length from the inside hinge wire piece about ½" (13mm) from the edge of the lid. Apply fresh clay to hold in place and blend with the inside of the lid. Tape with masking tape, if necessary, to hold in place, and allow to cure thoroughly. Place mixed, uncured clay over the wires to secure them in place. Allow to cure.

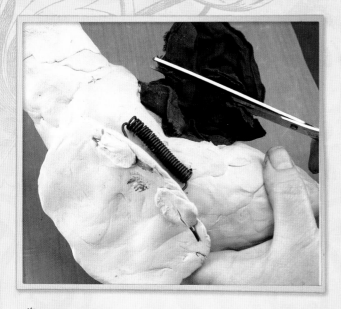

17. Cut away the excess silk lining leaving about 1½" (4cm) of excess all the way around the opening.

18. Begin gluing a layer of fabric, such as stretchy black velvet, on the outside body of the bird. This layer will be covered with several more layers here and there, so consider not using any expensive or special fabric for this step. The goal is to create a foundation to attach other fabrics and trim. Allow the glue to dry thoroughly.

19. Create a strap sewn from matching fabric(s) and hand-stitch it onto the bird body just outside of the lid.

20. Sew on larger buttons, crystal beads or found objects for the eyes. One possibility for a lid closure is to align buttons on the bird body with buttonhole loops sewn onto the lid. Gather several layers of beaded netting or tulle (or a bunch of actual feathers secured in some netting) and attach for a tail. Trim as desired.

Bees Knees Cocktail
Memorabilia Box

Once, during Prohibition, I was forced to live for days on nothing but food and water.

—W. C. Fields

I've always loved the idea of a speakeasy especially after visiting one on the Sacramento Delta. It had the coolest little door that they'd open to ask the secret password before opening the large door to let people in—just like in the Wizard of Oz! One day, I just happened to find the perfect door-within-a-door to use for this project while I was shopping at an antique store. I also found out while doing research about the Prohibition, that our favorite beach Whiskey Run served as a shipping point to distribute alcohol from Coos Bay, Oregon a.k.a., "Booze Bay." This area was the main exporter of alcohol to Washington, Oregon and California. Coos Bay was a booming lumber town back in the day, and large logs would be hollowed out to hide bottles of alcohol. Sneaky, sneaky.

What ties the elements of this project together are the bronzed leaves that come from the design on the door. The epoxy clay leaves have a faux finish that works well with the metal door insert. The leaves are used to attach the Prohibition photos, displayed on a piece from an old piano (a staple in speakeasies) and are mixed in with the found objects hanging from the spine of the altered book.

I also learned that mixed drinks became much more popular during the Prohibition. It wasn't a happy thing to drink nasty-tasting homemade alcohol and so other ingredients were mixed in to improve the flavor. The most popular expression back then for something oh-so-cool was *the bee's knees*. That saying came about because bees pack pollen in the middle of their legs, so it refers to where the good stuff is. Hence, the name for an imaginary cocktail and the name of this project.

Materials

decorative vintage box to house an altered journal you wish to house

silicone molding compound

unmixed epoxy clay

$1/16$" (2mm) drill bit

photocopies of several vintage photos

scissors

small embellishments to attach to the photos such as charms, bits of lace or pressed flowers

clear packing tape

fabric scraps to back the photos

craft glue

acrylic paint (your choice)

paintbrushes

metallic powder (your choice)

matte medium

alcohol ink: (your choice)

dowel or rod in the theme of your piece

18-gauge wire

wire cutters

metal file

epoxy glue

spring clip (optional)

assorted found objects and charms to suit your piece

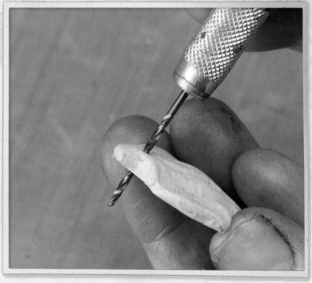

1. Choose a box with decorative designs to hold your finished altered journal. Make a silicone mold of a small decorative element found on the box. You can make several different molds and experiment with the design possibilities. Using the silicone mold(s), sculpt your decorative elements. Press the clay into each mold to sculpt it.

2. Poke a hole in the uncured clay pieces (which will be used for hanging them), using a ¼6" (2mm) drill bit. Set aside all the clay pieces to cure.

Inspired Tip

There are many sources online to find vintage images that are in the public domain.
Try searching for "public domain image" and whatever subject you are looking for in quotes.

3. Cut out the the vintage photos leaving a white border around each, if desired. Place a small, flat item (such as a coin, button or dried pressed flower) onto each photo. Then, apply clear packing tape over each photo, attaching the item, and encasing the photo in tape.

4. Cut a small piece of fabric slightly larger than the photos. Using craft glue, adhere a fabric piece to the back of each photo. Allow the glue to dry. Then trim the fabric so the edges are roughly flush with the edges of the photo.

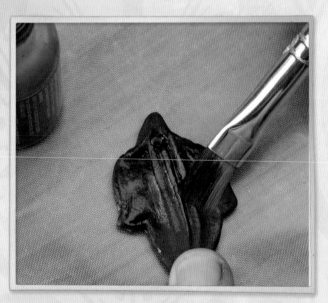

5. Add color to the clay pieces. Start by painting them with acrylic paint. Allow the paint to dry. Then mix metallic powder with matte medium and brush that over the paint. Finally, after that has dried, dab on some alcohol ink.

6. Choose a rod or dowel-shaped piece that ties in with your theme. (I used a part from an old piano because they were quite common in speakeasies.) Cut several 4" (10cm) lengths of 18-gauge wire—enough for each of your clay elements. Bend each piece of wire into a U shape and insert one wire through each element. Then bend the wire loosely around the rod and twist to close. Cut away any extra wire, and file if necessary, to prevent sharp ends (or bend the end of the wire back in on itself). Using an epoxy glue, attach one photo to each clay element. (It's helpful to clamp each photo to a clay element using a spring clip while the glue cures.)

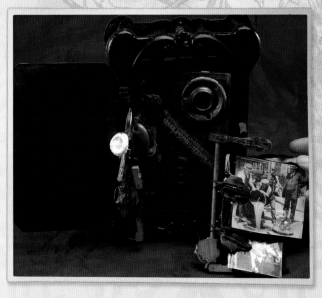

7. Attach a mix of the remaining clay elements and theme-related found objects to the spine of the altered book. This can be done with wire or with epoxy glue.

8. Display your pieces as you see fit.

From the Gallery

Broken Hearted
Beth Robinson

"Broken Hearted" was created for Valentine's Day. She has a wood base, a wire under-skirt, and is sculpted from epoxy clay.

Waxing Moon
Necklace

And it's something quite peculiar
Something shimmering and white
Leads you here despite your destination
Under the Milky Way tonight
— Steven Kilbey, Karin Jansson, "Under The Milky Way"
Performed by The Church

*T*he moon influences the tides and all water on earth, and can also profoundly affect our emotions and behavior; perhaps being as we are made mostly of water ourselves. We see the moon change from a crescent to a full circle and back again as different parts of the moon's sunlit surface are turned toward earth. I think of a new moon as earth's child born into darkness. As the new moon grows, we continue to see more of the sunlit side, which is known as a waxing moon. A half month later we see a full moon when all of the sunlit side is visible. To complete the cycle, more and more of the moon falls into shadow and this is a waning moon.

The Waxing Moon neckpiece stars all phases of the moon. If we wanted to sculpt perfectly round moons from clay alone, it would not be an easy task, even by a full moon's light. But a secret hidden inside each moon allows us to create a perfectly matched set, as all you readers of the Getting Started section (see page 8) can attest.

In the spirit of levity and mirth, you may wish to add either melted beeswax or wax medium to impart a waxy glow to your moons, especially those of the waxing persuasion. The rigid clay moons fully support encaustic layer(s) so this is a marriage made in, shall we say, the heavens.

Materials

- 1" (3cm) circle punch or template
- chipboard, medium weight
- unmixed epoxy clay
- nonstick craft sheet
- skewer, needle tool or similar tool to make channels in clay
- black waxed linen thread
- scissors
- texture plate or texture mold of your choosing
- acrylic paint: black, buttercream (off-white with a hint of yellow), burnt umber
- paintbrushes
- matte acrylic varnish
- beeswax and melting pot for wax
- dedicated paintbrush for wax
- thin strips of black lace
- paper towels
- clasp or other finding

1. Cut or punch out nine identical circles from a piece of medium-weight chipboard.

2. Press a pea-size ball of uncured clay into the center of each circle. With a slightly wet finger, spread the clay to the edges in a circular motion. Once the clay is covering the entire circle, use your finger to bevel the edges of the clay around the outside of the circle. Allow the clay to cure.

3. Flip all the circles over and repeat step 2 to cover the backsides with clay and bevel the edges. Before the clay cures, press a skewer or similar tool into the clay forming two parallel channels. Allow the clay to cure.

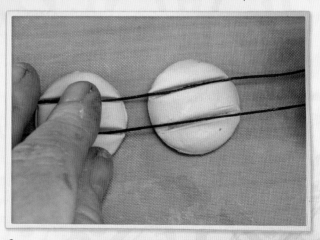

4. Place the nine circles about ½" (13mm) apart in a semicircular pattern (visualize how the necklace will look when worn) with the channels facing up. Run two lengths of linen thread through the channels of all nine circles.

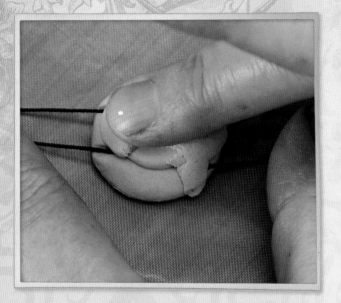

5. Apply a small amount of clay over the thread. You want the clay to go down into the channels far enough to hold both pieces of linen thread in place. If you have any trouble with the thread pulling back out of the pieces you've already covered, just do one circle at a time and wait for the clay to cure. Apply one final pea-sized ball of clay over the back of the circles and repeat the circular motions as in step 2.

6. Press a texture mold into the fresh clay on the back of the necklace and around the sides. Allow the clay to cure.

Inspired Tip

If you are not confident with the proportion sizes of the nine phases of the moon, there are numerous resources available online to help. Simply do a search for "phases of the moon" and you'll be presented wtih many images and sites.

7. Paint the backs of the circles with black acrylic paint and allow to dry. Apply a light coat of acrylic varnish and allow to dry.

Flip the necklace back to the front. Holding the thread out of the way, paint the circles with the phases of the moon (New Moon, Waxing Crescent, First Quarter, Waxing Gibbous, Full Moon, Waning Gibbous, Last Quarter, Waning Crescent and back to New Moon) from left to right using buttercream and black acrylic paints.

If the circle is mostly black (such as Waning Crescent), paint the circle black and then use a circle of chipboard as a mask to paint in a crescent with buttercream. It may take several coats to fully cover the black. If the circle is mostly buttercream, paint the entire circle buttercream and add black to it.

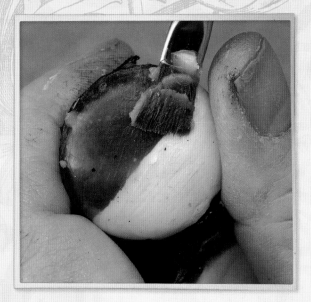

8. When all the moons are dry, take the paintbrush with the buttercream paint and dip it in water. Apply a very light wash over the black paint to give it the look of it being very dark but still visible in the night sky.

When the paint is fully dry, paint beeswax over the moons using one stroke over each color. Then apply a light coat of acrylic varnish to the surface of the wax. It will bead up, so repeatedly smooth the varnish over the surface of the wax until it adheres. Repeat with two or more additional coats of varnish.

Inspired Tip

Beeswax can be found online and at some art stores. It's available as pellets or in brick form. When using wax, you'll want to use a dedicated brush, as it's impossible to get all of the wax out of the bristles once you've used it for encaustic work. But it can be used over and over again with the wax. Melt beeswax in a small slow cooker (Crock-Pot) over low heat. When melted, brush the wax over each phase of the moon. Apply heat from a craft heat gun moving over the surface to fuse (smooth out) the wax. Often, dammar resin is mixed in with the wax but I don't like the fumes so I only use 100-percent beeswax.

9. Tie thin strips of black lace across the two threads in between each moon and also on the ends.

10. Apply a wash of watered-down burnt umber paint over the black paint on the back of the moons. Remove some of the paint with a paper towel. Allow it dry. Apply a final coat of varnish over the backs of the moons.

11. Determine how long you'd like the necklace to be and attach a clasp or other findings to finish. I tied on one extra black thread on either end of the necklace and braided the threads together. One end has a button and the other end has 3 holes for the button to go through thereby making the necklace adjustable from choker length to a short necklace.

Sacred Totem
Pedestal Art

In response to the question, "What is life?"

It is the flash of a firefly in the night.
It is the breath of a buffalo in the winter time.
It is the little shadow which runs across the grass
and loses itself in the sunset.

— Crowfoot, April 1890, on his deathbed

The significance of totems in various societies has been present through the centuries over much of the world. They were often a way to unify beliefs among tribes, and they were a way to share stories and common symbolism. Although totems have a serious side, there are many examples of unexpected humor, such as a face peering out from a whale's spout hole.

So here we have my version of a bird totem with both a serious side and a humorous side. The juxtaposition of these qualities is found in a lot of our art. It sometimes can be a bit dark or creepy, but there's often something lighthearted and quaint in the same piece to balance it out.

Using several molds makes this quite easy to put together. The dress form was free sculpted, although it would be easy to find one as these are quite common now. The bird skull looks especially believable, and the clay takes aging techniques in paint very well. As you'll see, the base of this project is the same as Through the Glass Darkly (page 96). If you make a mold of a base such as this, you can use it in so many ways, such as on a jewelry tree, supporting a glass candy dish, cake plate or a fish bowl.

Materials

silicone molding putty

papier-mâche bust or dress form

unmixed epoxy clay

curved mold or non-stick craft sheet

silicone mold for small feathers

18-gauge wire

wire cutters

drill and $^1/_{16}$" (2mm) drill bit

masking tape

paper clay

sewing pattern tissue

scissors

découpage medium

paintbrushes

acrylic paint (your choice, but include two shades of brown: one light, one dark)

silicone mold of a bird head or head of your choice (doll or animal)

silicone mold for a pedestal base (see page 96 for an example)

dowel in a width that will fit in the hole of the pedestal base with a little extra room

saw (to cut dowel)

thin found object (optional)

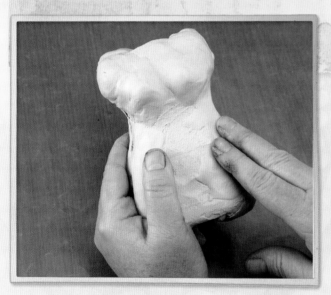

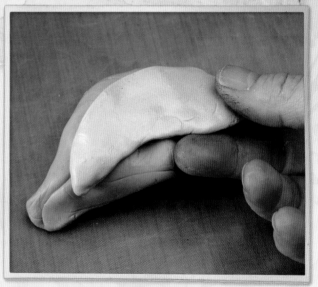

1. Using a silicone mold, sculpt a dress form shape using mixed clay. The mold should consist of a front and a back, which you can seam together with additional clay. This will allow the finished form to remain hollow, and you will need less clay than if you filled the mold solid. You don't need to spend a lot of time smoothing the clay—just a basic form will do. Leave an opening at the top and bottom of the form that will be large enough to accommodate your wood dowel.

2. Form two wings from mixed clay freehand by creating a flat wing shape. Drape the wing shapes over the back of a curved mold or on a nonstick craft sheet with a curved object underneath while the clay cures.

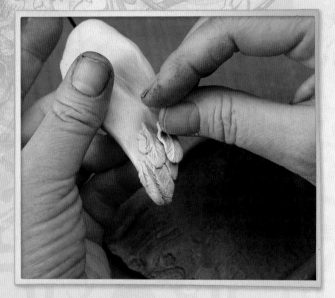

3. Using a mold of feathers, cast several small feather shapes. (The total number needed will depend on the size of your wing and the size of your feathers. I used approximately 25 feathers for each wing.) Apply the feathers to the wing shapes, using uncured clay, starting at the bottom and overlapping them as you work your way to the top.

4. Cut two pieces of 18-gauge wire about 4" (10cm). Attach one piece to the back of each wing, with about 3" (8cm) extending out of the wing. Add uncured clay to secure the wire to the wing. Allow all the clay to cure.

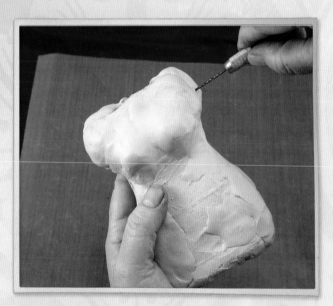

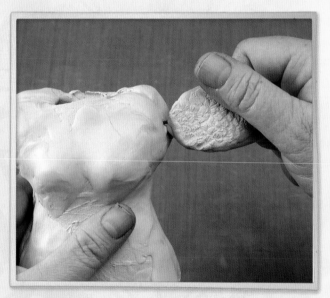

5. Drill two holes into the cured dress form, where you wish to add the wings, using a ¹⁄₁₆" (2mm) bit.

6. Add epoxy to the wire on one wing and to the edges of the wing around the wire. Insert the wire into one hole on the dress form. Repeat for the other wing on the other side. If you need a way of supporting the wings upright as the epoxy cures, use strips of masking tape.

84

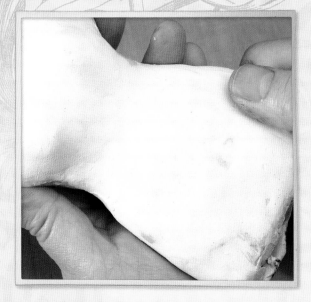

7. Cover the dress form with paper clay and smooth out the contour of the shape.

Inspired Tip

Paper clay works very well over an armature of epoxy clay. It's a quick-and-easy way to get a very smooth surface, and it's faster to smooth out than epoxy clay. I was delighted to have recently discovered a very strong paper clay formula that is made in Japan called Diamond Clay. (See Resources, page 124.)

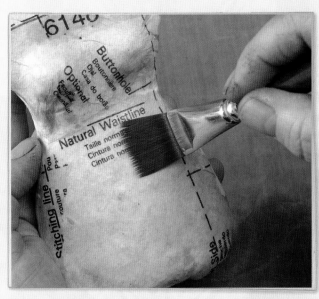

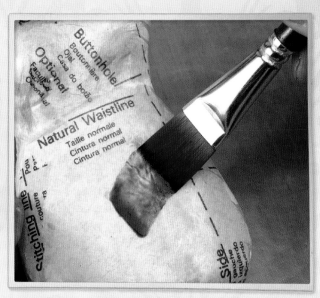

8. Cut strips of a sewing pattern tissue paper, and apply the tissue paper to the clay dress form using découpage (acrylic gel) medium. As you work, make use of interesting patterns or text on the paper, for example, placing "waistband" text over the waist portion of the form. When you are finished applying the paper, add a final coat of découpage medium, and allow the medium to dry.

9. Paint the dress form using a thin coat of acrylic paint (color of your choice). You can paint just a few areas of the dress form or the entire thing. Allow the paint to dry.

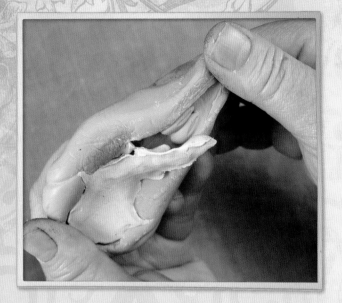

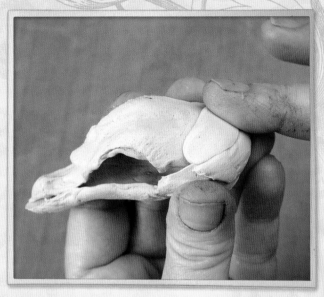

10. Using the silicone mold of a head (bird head, doll head, etc.) and mixed clay, sculpt the head for the totem.

11. If your skull is in two pieces, or you are missing a part of the skull and need to sculpt a portion of it by hand, attach the two pieces using additional clay, as needed. Make sure the clay is smooth.

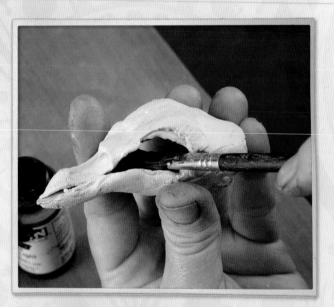

12. Using a dark shade of brown acrylic paint, apply a wash to the inside of the skull.

13. Apply a wash of a lighter shade of brown acrylic paint to the outside of the skull. Wipe the excess away and repeat a few times to get a beautifully subtle aged look. I like to rub the paint into the clay with my fingers a bit before wiping off the excess.

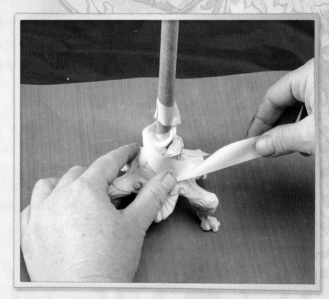

14. Using the silicone mold for your pedestal base, cast the shape from the necessary amount of mixed, uncured clay and allow the clay to cure.

Cut the wooden dowel to the required height. (Determine this by stacking all the elements and measuring the height.) Insert some uncured clay into the hole of the pedestal, then insert the wooden dowel into the clay in the cavity.

15. Place the pedestal base on a level surface and adjust the dowel so that it is straight. Wrap masking tape around both pieces to hold the dowel in place, if needed. Allow the clay to cure. Keep an eye on it as it cures and adjust as needed. (Remove the tape after the clay has cured.)

16. Paint the pedestal with acrylic paint, as desired. Allow the paint to dry. Stack all the elements on the dowel. Adding a thin found object between the dress form and head is a nice touch. Attach the head to the top of the dowel using a bit of uncured clay to hold it in place. Set aside to cure.

Edison Lamp Works
Light Fixture

We now know a thousand ways not to build a light bulb.
—Thomas Alva Edison

How exciting it must have been to have invented as many things as Edison and his team did. He invested in as many tools and instruments as he could afford, thereby creating an environment that would ultimately lead to so many profound successes at the Edison Lamp Works. Through his work in 1878 and 1879, Edison built an entire infrastructure for supporting the use of light bulbs, which included a way to meter electricity, generators and the cables required to connect everything together.

Today we are able to acquire Edison-style bulbs and can make very convincing reproductions of old-time lighting. Or, make more whimsical lighting such as this one with Edison's portrait as a young man displayed under an optical glass lens to pay homage to this great inventor.

This project was made to look very different from any historical lamp designs, yet still has a vintage look. This should give you several ideas of ways to make hanging lamps as well as table lamps and perhaps even floor models (think PVC or copper pipe embellished with ornate designs in clay applied to the surface).

Materials

- vintage light feature with lenses
- silicone molding compound
- lenses to fit newly-cast pieces from mold
- unmixed epoxy clay, black (Apoxie Sculpt)
- awl or pin vise with $1/16$" (2mm) bit

- black beading thread and needle
- black matte beads
- hurricane lamp cover
- black waxed linen thread
- scissors
- computer with photo-editing software

- images of Thomas Edison edited to fit within the confines of your lens size
- printer
- transparency film for printer
- jewelry glue (Diamond Glaze)
- lamp socket to fit hurricane

1. Create a silicone mold from a preexisting light fixture. This might include several different pieces, but should include at least one part that is meant to house a lens. Fit a magnifying lens into the silicone mold you made.

2. Sculpt black, mixed clay around the glass using the pattern on the mold. The clay should be attached to, but not covering, the glass.

3. When the clay has partially cured, remove the clay-and-glass piece from the mold and make a hole in the top center, using an awl or a pin vise with a ¼6" (2mm) bit. Using the same bit, also make a hole at the two top corners on the sides of the piece. Repeat steps 1–2 to create two more pieces of clay, placing holes at identical spots on all three pieces. Allow all of the clay pieces to cure.

4. Attach the three pieces with strands of black matte beads so that they fit around the glass fixture. The pieces should be connected at the top with three lengths of beads that are about 3" (8cm) long. Thread the needle from the back of the top center hole to the front of the piece, thread on a bead, then go back through the hole and begin threading on enough beads for the next 3" (8cm) length. To connect the sides, use the same method, but use longer strands to allow the beads to drape and tie them off at each corner.

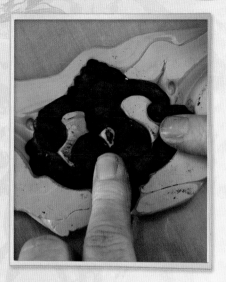

5. Drape the three lenses with attached beaded strands over the hurricane glass fixture.

6. Sculpt three ornate pieces from a second silicone mold. Press black, mixed clay into the mold, being careful to leave the appropriate negative space in spots (see Best Method for Filling a Mold, page 13.)

7. When the pieces are partially cured, gently remove them from the mold and bend them to fit the curve of the glass fixture. Leave them to cure on a surface that will support the curve.

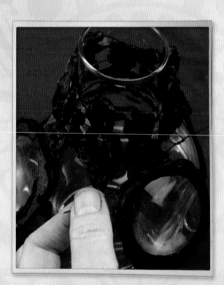

8. Using black waxed linen thread, attach the three ornate curved clay pieces between and slightly overlapping the lens pieces. If you wish, you could use mixed, uncured clay to connect them as well.

9. Print out three images of Edison's portrait (or other image of your choice) onto transparency film. Cut out the images to the shape of the lenses. Using a bit of clear glue (such as jewelry glue) around the edges of the tranparency circle, attach the images to the insides of the lenses.

10. Bring the cord of the lamp socket up through the bottom of the glass fixture until the socket comes to rest against the glass.

Savoy
Liz Mcgrath

wood, foam, resin, cloth,
acrylic paint
2007
42" x 22" x 22"

Deerhouse
Liz Mcgrath

wood, foam,
resin, cloth,
acrylic paint
2007
37" x 20" x 12"

Reliquary of Fishes
Aquarium

fish die belly upward, and rise to the surface. It's their way of falling.

—André Gide

*L*ike so many pieces I've made, this fish tank is tied to an adventure with an artist friend. My husby, Charley, and I were garage saling and we were finding some awesome sales. So I called my friend, Rachel Whetzel, to make sure she knew about these great deals. We met up at one of the sales where we both immediately spied the coolest heavy glass containers. They were actually old battery cases, and this was the first time I'd ever seen one. I thought the price was a little high so I reluctantly passed.

After a delightful lunch with Rachel and her sons, she surprised me with one of the glass containers! I knew right then it was going in the book. The great thing about this epoxy clay is it's safe to use in aquariums and in zoos! Some enterprising artists are making a living creating custom marine environments using this clay. And, it is strong enough to hold and support this heavy container, filled with water, up off the table high enough to allow a light to slip underneath for a really striking effect. You might even add some sort of sculpture inside so that the fishies can enjoy it too.

Materials

- silicone molding compound
- decorative elements to cast from, including something like a furniture claw foot and also some type of scroll work
- unmixed epoxy clay
- large glass container

- tinfoil
- masking tape
- nonstick craft sheets, 2
- rolling pin or similar
- steel-edge ruler
- craft knife
- clay shaper tool
- acrylic paints: your choice

- paintbrushes
- uplight (optional)
- disposable wipes
- gravel or clear glass pebbles and/or clear marbles
- aquatic plants
- fish-friendly sculpture (optional)

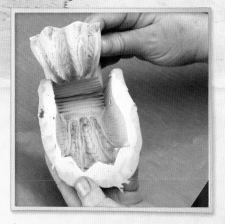

1. Create a silicone mold for what will become the feet of the fish tank. I used a claw shape from a piece of old furniture. When pushing the clay into the mold, the shape can remain hollow inside the sides of the shape—it need not fill the mold entirely. You will also need to create molds for additional decorative elements. Sculpt four "feet" from the silicone mold using mixed, uncured clay. Allow the pieces to cure.

2. Flip the fish tank container over and cover the bottom with tinfoil. (Tape the foil, if desired, to hold it in place while working.) Apply mixed, uncured clay over the foil at the four corners, creating a type of L shape. You will need about a golf-ball amount of mixed clay for each corner, and the shaped clay should be about ½" (13mm) thick. Then, build up a "shelf" of clay along the sides, connecting the corners. This shelf is what will hold the glass tank, so use at least ½" (13mm) thickness of clay all around.

3. Attach the feet to the uncured clay at the corners by pushing them into the clay and positioning them at a 45-degree angle. Allow the clay to cure.

Inspired Tip
Since there is a large amount of clay used in this project, it is easier to mix up individual batches of clay and apply it in sections as you go.

Inspired Tip
If your base will have a light element inside, plan to use enough clay to raise the container high enough to clear whatever light you will be using. Keep the light with you for reference. Also plan to leave an opening in the base if you don't want to have to lift the aquarium to change the light and/or turn it on if the switch is located on the light itself. This aquarium is designed to slide or pull the light out through an opening in the back of the base.

  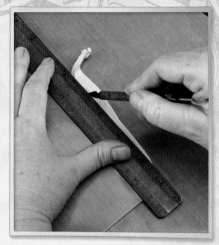

4. Once the shelf is made, create a clay veneer to go over it. Flatten a piece of newly mixed clay into a sheet roughly the length and width of one side of the shelf, onto a nonstick craft sheet.

5. Roll out the sheet to an even width with a rolling pin or similar item (and a second nonstick craft sheet.)

6. Trim the edges of the rolled clay to give a finished look. Position the craft sheet along the line you'd like to cut. Place the steel-edged ruler along the same line. Trim the edges with a craft blade being careful not to cut or scratch the surface of the craft sheet underneath.

7. Gently press the clay veneer sheet onto the part of the clay shelf that shows. Texture the clay veneer sheet with a silicone texture sheet and blend into the surrounding areas if necessary.

Using the silicone molds created at the beginning, sculpt several decorative pieces to embellish the tank. You'll want one element repeated in each of the four corners, and another element to span the center of each of the four sides. I used the same mold to create different pieces. Some I left whole and flat, while others I cut down and bent to curve. Note that some of the decorative clay elements use the entire mold and others have only used a portion of the mold. Keep these options in mind when laying out your design.

8. Place a nonstick craft sheet over the corner of the glass container and tape in place. Take castings out of the mold(s) you have chosen after the clay has begun to set up and isn't as sticky but well before it is fully cured (see page 10, States of Clay). Bend the casting around the corner and tape in place being careful not to distort the ornate design of the casting. Allow to fully cure and repeat for all decorative elements that are to follow a curve.

9. On three sides of the tank, apply additional clay, connecting to the four corners, to form a solid base. This is what will hold up the glass container so be sure the base is thick, sturdy and solid. Paint as desired. Here, I wanted a patina look, so I used a variety of blue and green hues.

10. Place your decorative elements onto the glass container based on your predetermined layout by pressing firmly onto the container evenly from side to side. Trim away the clay that comes out from the edges of the decorative elements, using a craft knife.

11. Smooth and blend the clay with a silicone clay shaper tool, then wipe away any clay residue from the glass surface, using a disposable wipe. Allow the clay to fully cure. Elements can be painted prior to attaching them to the glass, or after—whichever you prefer.

12. If you've designed your aquarium to allow an uplight to slide into place, position it now. Carefully set the glass container down onto the base. It is now ready to add clear glass marbles to act as gravel (thereby allowing the uplight to shine through), aquatic plants and any fish-friendly sculpture you'd like to add.

Inspired Tip

Here are some fun design ideas:
- Create a lid for your tank.
- Create a fish-friendly sculpture for inside the tank.
- Attach a magnifying glass (with a decorative clay handle of course!) to hang from the side to be used when viewing the fish.

Through the Glass Darkly
Standing Mirror

for now we see through a glass, darkly; but then face to face: now I know in part; but then shall I know even as also I am known.

—1 Corinthians 13:12

*T*his project—like many in this book—is one that is quite easy to make but looks impressively difficult. You don't even need to cut the mirror yourself as this can be done quite inexpensively at your local glass shop. Instead of a footed base made from clay, you could use any number of objects for an interesting look, such as the base of a kerosene lamp. Any glass lamp base would be fabulous with a bit of silver leaf applied sparsely over the glass and on the mirror, or any small sculptural piece with a sturdy base.

Let your imagination run wild both before and while working on this piece, and you'll be well rewarded with a most interesting and unique addition to your boudoir.

Materials

footed type of base to cast a mold from

decorative elements to cast press molds from

silicone molding putty

craft knife

unmixed epoxy clay

masking tape

wood dowel

saw (for cutting dowel to length)

nonstick craft sheet

oval mirror (standard size, or have a glass shop cut one for you from a pattern you bring in)

16-gauge wire

unmixed epoxy clay, black (Apoxie Sculpt)

wire cutters

clay tool (optional)

round-nose pliers

black fabric of your choice large enough to cover back of mirror

craft glue

scissors

elements to embellish mirror (chain, found objects, crystal links)

 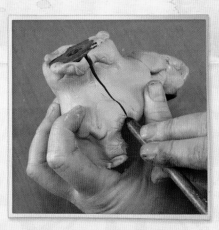 

1. Begin by creating a silicone mold from which you will sculpt the pedestal base of the mirror. You will need an object that will be sturdy enough to support a dowel and mirror. The object I'm casting from here is an actual mirror base. (For more on using silicone putty, see page 12.) Also, you will need to make a mold of a small decorative element (see step 8).

2. Once the silicone has cured, carefully slice the mold down one side.

3. Slowly and gently remove the cured mold from the object.

4. Fill the mold with freshly mixed clay leaving a hole at the top. If the mold starts to pull open where you cut it, tape the mold shut tightly by wrapping it several times with masking tape. Allow to fully cure. Note: To begin this project, I used regular (white) epoxy clay and later painted it black, but for the remaining elements, I switched to using black clay, which saved me from having to paint it later.

Cut a length of wooden dowel rod to a length where, when standing upright in your base, it will end 1" (3cm) beyond where you want the bottom of the mirror to hit. Fill the cavity of the cured base piece with fresh clay and push the dowel down about 1" (3cm) into the clay. Blend the clay to smooth with the cured clay.

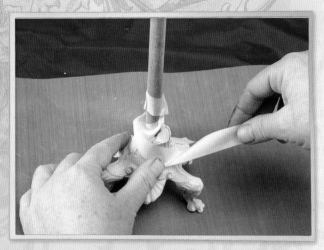

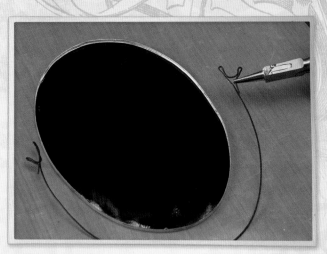

5. Place the pedestal base on a level surface and adjust the dowel so that it is straight. Wrap masking tape around both pieces to hold it in place, if needed. Allow the clay to cure. Keep an eye on it as it cures and adjust as needed. (Remove the tape after the clay has cured.)

6. Lay the mirror on a nonstick craft sheet. Using the curved form as a guide, bend a length of wire (about 24" [61cm]) to form the same curve shaped; the wire should follow just the bottom half of the mirror. On each end of the wire, bend 2" (5cm) into a rabbit ear shape with a little extra tail. This will support the mirror.

7. Cover the wire with black mixed clay. Stop adding clay just below the rabbit ears but do cover the sharp tails.

8. Using a mold, if desired, sculpt two decorative elements to enhance the design of the mirror. Also sculpt a piece for the handle of the mirror. Place identical elements on the back in the same places, if desired.

9. Cut a piece of fabric slightly larger than the mirror. Adhere to the back of the mirror with craft glue. Use enough glue to firmly adhere the fabric but not so much that it saturates the fabric. When the glue dries, trim the excess fabric around the mirror, using scissors.

10. Add a coil of mixed clay around the perimeter of the mirror to form a frame. Use a clay tool or your finger and a bit of water to smooth the edges and keep the surface looking neat. Add another decorative element on the bottom of the mirror to act as a handle when the mirror is removed from the base.

11. Bend a 5" (13cm) piece of wire into a U shape. At about 1" (3cm) from the loop, bend the remaining wire out 90 degrees and curve to fit the contour of the mirror. Embed the wire into the side of the mirror with freshly mixed clay, in the center of the mirror's side. Repeat at the same location on the opposite side of the mirror and allow to fully cure.

12. Bend a 3" (8cm) piece of wire into a U shape and then into a hook. Attach the wire hook to the back of the clay mirror support to hang embellishments. Repeat on the other side and allow to fully cure.

13. Add beaded chain, charms, found objects, chains of crystals and anything else that strikes your fancy onto the hooks. If they don't all fit on the hooks, you can attach them with jump rings to chain already hanging from the hooks. Alternatively, you can make larger hooks but I kept mine smaller so as not to be noticeable from the front.

14. Place the mirror down on the base by placing the wire extensions attached to the mirror into the wire supports on the base. You can now use the mirror on the base or remove it and use as a hand mirror.

Requiem of Undying Love
Coatrack

See! on yon drear and rigid bier low lies thy love, Lenore!
Come! let the burial rite be read—the funeral song be sung!—
An anthem for the queenliest dead that ever died so young—
A dirge for her the doubly dead in that she died so young.

—from "Lenore" by Edgar Allen Poe

I like to imagine Edgar having cherished this shadow box, holding remembrances of Lenore's life—her name long ago stitched onto a linen heart, edged with lace trim. Along with a remnant of his beloved's gown—now in tatters—these mementos are ever with him as a memory and a deep sorrow even to the point of madness . . . .

Flanked by stoic ravens, this piece is both a tribute to Edgar's prose and a functional coatrack, suitable to greet guests with the unusual as they enter your dwelling to escape tempestuous gales on a bleak December night.

Epoxy clay is used in many different ways for this project. The glass in the shadow box is supported by a ring of clay around the inside so that it cannot move. The glass is also adhered to the shadow box with the clay. The armature under the ravens is made from aluminum foil and clay. Finally, the chains and crystals that unite the three pieces are held in place with wire holders secured with clay for strength.

Materials

lightweight tinfoil (not heavy-duty)

unmixed epoxy clay

18-gauge wire

wire cutters

paper clay

nonstick craft sheet

acrylic paints: black, burnt umber, off-white

paintbrushes

oval piece of glass

foam core (large enough to trace glass onto)

pencil

craft knife

chipboard

ruler

masking tape

tissue paper

découpage medium

heat gun (optional)

awl or needle tool

Edgar Allen Poe transparency

muslin

lace trim

craft glue

memorabilia to represent "Lenore"

Create the Ravens

1. Begin by creating the foil base for the clay raven. Start with a form for the beak.

2. Continue adding foil to create the shape of the head and the start of the neck.

3. Round out the shape until you have a finished form you are happy with.

4. Place a larger patch of mixed clay on the back of the raven. Create a wire hanger from a piece of 18-gauge wire, cut to about 3" (8cm) and bend into a U shape. Hold the hanger in place with additional clay. Allow to fully cure.

5. Apply mixed, uncured clay to the entire foil bird form. Allow the clay to cure. Cover the clay bird with a layer of paper clay to provide a smoother surface. (Do not cover the wire hanger.) After the paper clay is dry, paint the bird with black acrylic paint. When dry, brush over the top with watered-down, burnt umber wash.

Repeat steps 1–5 to create a second bird. Set the raven heads aside while you create the shadow box.

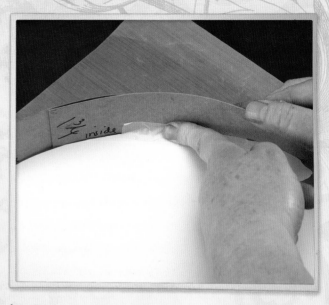

6. Trace your oval piece of glass onto the foam core and cut it out using a sharp craft knife. Cut several strips of chipboard to a width of 2" (5cm). Attach the strips of chipboard to the foam core with masking tape, resting the chipboard on top of the foam core.

7. Stagger the seams where the strips meet. Continue attaching strips until the entire perimeter of the box has sides that are two thicknesses of chipboard.

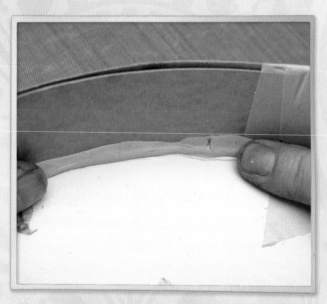

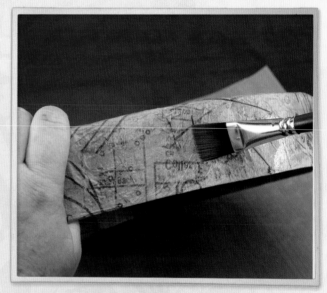

8. Apply snakes of freshly mixed clay on the inside and outside seam where the foam core meets the chipboard.

9. Cover the entire inside and outside of the box (foam core and cardstock strips) with several layers of tissue applied with découpage medium. Allow each layer to dry thoroughly before applying the next. (Note: The layers will dry very quickly if dried with a craft heat gun.) It is not necessary to wait for the clay (from step 8) to cure first if you are careful to not disturb it too much when gluing the tissue. The clay will continue to cure as you work.

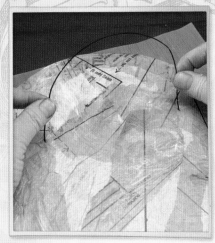

10. Cut a length of 18-gauge wire to 12" (31cm). Create two holes about 4" (10cm) apart in the back, using an awl or needle tool, about one-fourth of the way down from the top. Bend the wire into a large open U shape and, working from the outside of the box to the inside, put one end of the wire through each hole.

11. Leave enough of the U on the back to act as a hanger and bend the wires to lay flat on the inside. Secure with snakes of freshly rolled clay to completely cover the wire. Apply masking tape to hold in place until the clay is cured, if necessary.

12. Poke a set of holes 2" (5cm) apart on each side of the box, about ½" (13mm) down from the back edge and about one-fourth of the way up from the bottom of the box. Cut two lengths of 18-gauge wire to 6" (15cm). Bend each wire into a U shape and put each end through one hole leaving about ½" (13mm) of the U on the outside.

Bend the wire tails along the curve inside the box and attach with snakes of freshly mixed clay to form hangers for chains that will attach to the ravens. Apply masking tape to hold the wire in place until the clay is cured. Cover the clay areas with more paper layers.

Create the Lid

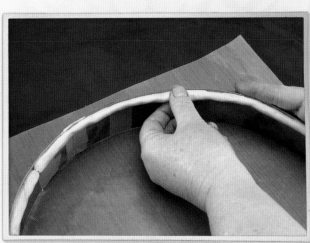

13. Cut strips of chipboard 1" (3cm) wide. Tape the strips together with masking tape, staggering the seams, like you did for the box. Use the outside diameter of the box as a guide to ensure you make the lid fit over the box. It should be large enough to slide easily over the box. Roll snakes of freshly mixed clay and apply along one edge of the lid, keeping it closer to the inside. Blend the clay together for a consistent look and allow to fully cure. The clay will create a lip for the glass to sit against.

14. As you did for the box, cover the lid with paper and découpage medium. Check periodically to make sure the lid still fits easily onto the base.

15. Place the clay edge side of the lid facedown on a large sheet of craft paper. Trace around the exterior of the lid to create a paper pattern. Using the pattern as a guide, cut an oval shape of glass or take to your local glass shop.

Paint the top and bottom pieces of the shadow box in the acrylic color of your choice. Allow all clay to cure and paint to dry.

16. Place the lid with the clay edge faceup and carefully lay the glass down on the lid. Once the edges are aligned, apply snakes of freshly mixed clay around the front of the glass and down onto the sides of the lid. Blend the clay together and then trim the clay around the glass with a craft blade, if necessary. Clean any clay residue from the glass and allow to fully cure.

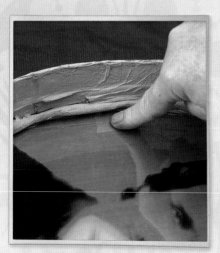

17. Trim the Edgar transparency to fit inside the lid. Place the side of the transparency with the ink up against the glass to protect it from getting scratched. Apply snakes of freshly mixed clay along the inside seam where the glass meets the sides of the lid. Blend and trim the clay if needed, clean any clay residue from the glass and allow the clay to fully cure.

18. Arrange vintage lace around the sides and edges of the glass. Glue the lace in place using craft glue and add other trims as desired.

19. Loosely arrange background fabric on the inside of the shadow box and glue in place with craft glue. Add additional layers of fabrics and other embellishments.

Place the lid on the box and seal with a snake of mixed clay. Paint the cured clay to match the rest of the box. Hang the box on the wall, and hang one raven on each side of the box to act as hooks.

From the Gallery

Coming Out of the Dark
Esther Verschoor

"Coming out of the dark is made of Aves Apoxie sculpt and a Lovebird skull.

"She represents the courage that one of my collectors found to come out of the darkness in her life and stepping into the sunlight to enjoy life."

Alan Rogerson
bathroom

"When I'm not carving wax for custom jewelry, I will be painting, sculpting or tattooing. It took me over 3 years to sculpt over and paint my bathroom. Sculpting epoxy allows me to realize ideas that I otherwise can't imagine how to make."

Well Dressed Table
Altered Condiment Set

failure is the condiment that gives success its flavor.

—Truman Capote

An antique condiment set with an ornate design and matching bottles can easily run into the hundreds. But I've bought several of these with mismatched bottles and some broken or missing pieces for much less. This one was twenty dollars at a garage sale down the road. In this fun project, we can rewrite history by adding elements that weren't ever used together in such a convincing way that most likely only an antiques dealer would question its authenticity.

This project shows how thinking outside the box can make something magical. For the arms extending out to hold the saltcellars, a mold

from an antique floor lamp had the perfect ornate design that would work well with an existing item from the Victorian era. Little bird heads with seashell flourishes were adhered to faceted crystal balls to replace the long-lost lids on some of the bottles. Of course epoxy clay doesn't look like the silver-plated pieces so the solution is to apply silver leaf with a very easy and fun "aging" recipe to blend everything together in a most convincing way.

Materials

condiment set (less-than-perfect condition is fine)

molds of an ornate floor lamp arm, chandelier arm or similar, 2

mold of a bird head or whatever you'd like to use for lid

mold of an ornate shape to form the "bobeche" (holds the saltcellars)

mold of seashells or similar to go around bird's neck

unmixed epoxy clay

silver leaf and adhesive

paintbrushes

nonstick craft sheet

clay shaper tool

beads or other embellishments

small faceted lead crystal balls

aging art supplies (brown and black acrylic paint, acrylic matte varnish,

wax medium, alcohol inks and dry pigment)

masking tape

silver-colored belt, necklaces, strands of crystal, etc.

small containers to act as saltcellars (small crystal bowls, miniature silver tart pans, etc.)

small spoons to fit in the saltcellars

Before You Begin

Using the three-dimensional, ornate arm molds, create two clay arms and allow to cure (see Making Double-Sided, 3-D Molds on page 16.) For the ornate arms that will hold the saltcellars, I made a mold from parts of an antique floor lamp. You will also need to make a dimensional mold, which will be used to sculpt the stoppers for the saltshakers. I used small faceted lead crystal balls as the actual stoppers and attached silver-leafed and aged clay birds as lid handles. Finally, make a mold to serve as a decorative piece where the arms will be attached. This will cover some not-so-pretty clay used to attach the two ornate arms to the condiment set.

Here is a typical, plain condiment set. The containers don't all match and there are pieces missing.

1. To make lids to replace missing ones, sculpt mixed, uncured clay in the bird head mold. Attach sculpted clay embellishments, such as shell shapes, around the neck of the bird head. Blend the edges of the clay from the shell pieces in with the rest of the bird head. Flare the shells outward slightly and allow the clay to cure.

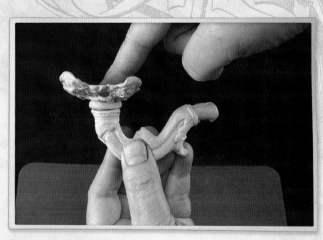

2. Following the manufacturer's instructions, apply silver-leaf adhesive over the entire surface of the bird head and apply the silver leaf. Place some unmixed clay onto a nonstick craft sheet. (Positioning the lead crystal ball onto the unmixed clay will hold it in place for the remaining steps.) Place some freshly mixed clay on the pointy part of the faceted lead crystal ball. Push the bird element down onto the clay to adhere it to the crystal ball. Blend the clay, if necessary, with a clay shaper tool so that it doesn't show. Leave the unmixed clay, crystal ball and bird element on the craft sheet and allow to cure. Repeat these steps for any additional lids that are needed for the condiment containers.

3. Attach a clay "bowl" to one of the sculpted arms, using a small bit of mixed clay. To create the "bowl," sculpt a small decorative element and curve it into a shape that will support one of your small chosen crystal bowls.

4. Attach shell embellishments at the seam where the arm meets the bowl and blend with a clay shaper tool. Alternately, you can impress beads or other items into this seam, and once the clay cures, it will be permanently attached. Repeat these steps for the other arm.

5. Apply silver-leaf adhesive and silver leaf to both arms and allow to dry. Apply aging techniques to the silver leaf as described in the tip on this page. Adhere the arms to the handle of the condiment set with freshly mixed clay.

Inspired Tip

Here are some aging techniques to use with silver leaf:

First, apply mixture of acrylic matte varnish and brown acrylic paint. After painting over all the surface, gently rub off any excess with a disposable wipe, leaving a residue on the surface. Apply a mixture of matte varnish and black acrylic paint in random areas and gently rub off those as well.

Dap on a mixture of matte varnish and a small amount of Pearl Ex Antique Silver powder in a random manner. Gently rub off, leaving a trace on the surface. Repeat with Pearl Ex Antique Gold powder.

6. Once you have the arm positioned, apply masking tape right over the freshly mixed clay and around the handle to hold it in place. Allow to fully cure and then remove the masking tape.

7. Repeat for the other arm. With some freshly mixed clay, attach a decorative element (that has been silver-leafed and aged) in the middle of the two arms to hide where the clay was used to attach them.

8. Blend the clay in and paint with silver paint or apply more silver leaf to blend in all the elements. (Note: You can paint raw clay and it will not affect it curing.) Apply another decorative element on the backside.

9. Place the containers into the holes and then place the bird lids on. Add the glass elements to act as saltcellars. Here I've used found objects that are small glass bowls. (Alternatively, you can use a glass bobeche with a small tart pan inside so the salt doesn't run out the hole.) Finally, apply a silver belt or other embellishment with freshly mixed clay. Apply masking tape to hold it in place and allow to fully cure.

Inspired Tip

Not all the salt shakers need to have clay stoppers. Use other crystals, found lid stoppers, glass radio tubes (for more of a steampunk look) or any found objects to embellish the lids. Also, if you will be using this set to actually serve condiments make sure any pieces are suitable for contact with food.

Memory Theater
Display Cabinet

One need not be a chamber to be haunted;
One need not be a house;
The brain has corridors surpassing
Material place.

—Emily Dickinson
"Time and Eternity"

Cabinets of Curiosity, or wunderkammer, were all the rage in Victorian times. Specimens from nature, religious relics, curiosities and even contrived hoaxes held the fascination and adoration of the Victorians.

These collections remind me of a favorite place I'd go when I was younger named Coyote Point. I loved that I could ride my bike so far from home and end up at such a magical place—at least it seemed to be magical and to be such a long journey at the time. A natural history museum there had many of the same items that were displayed in these old Victorian cabinets—shells of all shapes, colors and sizes, a huge Alaskan King Crab that spanned across an entire wall and curious items hidden from view in boxes that you could reach inside while trying to guess what they might be.

The initial idea for this project was to re-create a traditional wunderkammer but, as often happens, the influence of my dreams was a far greater influence. So in place of a collection of real speci-

mens from nature, this cabinet features a creature that could never be—except in dreams.

There are so many possibilities with this project. Any fanciful design can be combined and/or assembled into an "outline" for the shape of a cabinet. Glass is cut in the shape to fit the design of the clay and reinforced foam core pieces (or wood, if you have the tools) with the same pattern are the perfect recipe for a unique cabinet. And no worries if you don't feel comfortable cutting complex shapes. Most local glass shops will do this work for you quite inexpensively. Even window glass looks amazing when embellished with ornate designs in clay.

Epoxy clay adheres to the glass easily, so all you need to do is to clean up the edges a bit. Add an inexpensive light element to highlight a Victorian naturalist specimen, a collection of the rare and unusual, an art doll or anything of a curious nature to create a treasured focal point in your favorite space. It can become for you an artful reminder of everyday magic.

Materials

antique decorative (carved) frame or panel

silicone molding compound

unmixed epoxy clay, black (Apoxie Sculpt)

nonstick craft sheet

craft knife

glass to fit frame

kraft paper (for a pattern)

scissors

foam core

glass cutter (optional)

masking tape

tissue paper

découpage medium

acrylic paint (optional)

paintbrush

crystal-making supplies: silicone molding paste, silicone molding compound,

clear resin, mixing cups and craft stick

18-gauge wire

wire cutters

square-jawed pliers

window screening

24-gauge wire

32-gauge wire

needle and thread

chipboard

texture mold

assorted found-object embellishments

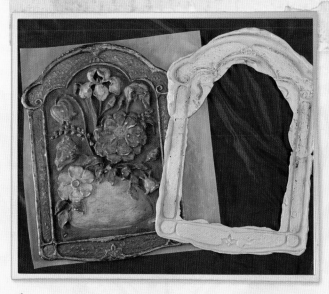

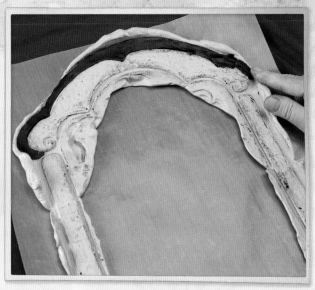

1. Find a dimensionally carved frame or piece of art with a shape that appeals to you. I chose this decorative piece because of its curved shape and the open spaces between the raised designs. Make a silicone mold frame from your piece that mimics a frame.

2. Start pressing small amounts of mixed clay into the mold.

3. Use a craft blade to clean up the edges of the clay. (Be sure to keep the blade running along the edge of the mold rather than down into the silicone.) Running the blade along the sides will make a huge difference in the finished piece so don't skip this step! Allow the clay to cure, but do not remove it from the mold.

4. Roll out about a golf-ball size of mixed clay into several small snake shapes. Place the snakes on top of the cured clay frame (which is still in the mold). Gently but firmly press the glass against the fresh clay. Flip the glass, clay and mold "sandwich" over so that the glass sheet is on your work surface. Start at one end and slowly remove the mold.

Then press the cured clay frame down on the glass sheet to secure it to the frame. Clay will be pushed out the sides. Use a craft blade to trim away any areas where the fresh clay comes out farther than the edge of the molded clay. If there are sections where there are gaps between the clay and the glass sheet, you can use the craft blade to push more clay underneath. Allow the fresh clay to cure.

5. Using the original piece as a guide, make a paper pattern of the contours of the piece. You will use this as a guide for cutting the back of the cabinet and also the glass front. (Note: You can make the cabinet taller than the original piece you make the mold from; just adjust the size of your pattern as needed.)

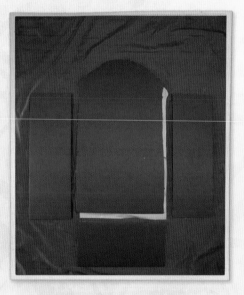

6. Using the pattern as a guide, cut foam core to create the back of the cabinet. Then cut out foam core pieces for the sides (two of the same piece) and bottom of the cabinet. Also use the pattern to cut a piece of glass for the front of the cabinet. (Note: If you don't know how to use a glass cutter, take the paper pattern piece to a local glass shop to have the glass cut.)

Inspired Tip

Clean any clay or clay residue off the glass right away with disposable wipes. Once the clay is cured, it can be cleaned more thoroughly with window cleaner.

7. Assemble the back, sides and bottom of the cabinet into a box shape, and add just enough masking tape to hold the pieces together.

    To make the box sturdy, cover the entire inside and outside of the box with several layers of tissue paper applied with découpage medium. Allow each layer to dry thoroughly before applying the next. (You can use a tissue paper color that is close to the color of the cabinet to save on painting.) Add extra layers at the seams to reinforce them. Then paint over the tissue paper with acrylic paint, if desired.

8. Attach crystals or other embellishments to the glass, as desired (see how to make your own crystals on page 14.) Then attach the glass front to cabinet. Set the foam core box with the back on the work surface. Then position the glass sheet on the top. Using a golf-ball size of mixed clay, attach the glass to the cabinet on both the inside and outside with the clay. Blend the clay with your fingers and water so that it's less visible. Remember, the glass needs to be firmly secured to the box. Allow the clay to cure.

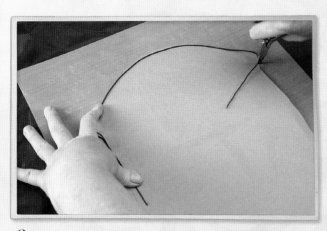

9. I originally thought about creating a door in the back of the cabinet to access the light inside, but then came up with the idea to make the entire cabinet accessible from the top. In order to do this, I made the top so it could pulled off.

    Using the paper pattern you cut for the glass as a guide, bend some 18-gauge steel wire to follow the contour of the top of the cabinet. The length of the wire that extends vertically down the sides of the pattern should equal one-half the depth of the cabinet plus 1" (3cm). This section of wire is going to be bent to extend along the cabinet sides. Repeat to form a second wire.

10. Place one of the wires from the previous step at the top of the back of the cabinet with masking tape, aligning the curves of the cabinet back with the curves of the wire. The wire should also be to the inside, as shown. Tape the other wire to the inside of the glass front with masking tape also, aligning the curves.

    Using square-jawed pliers, bend the excess wire from both pieces at a 45-degree angle so that they meet up and overlap on both sides. Attach the wires to each other by wrapping them together tightly with 24-gauge wire to form a frame.

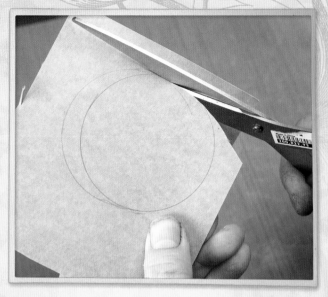

11. Cut a strip of screen cloth or other stiff open weave material of your choice so that it overlaps the wire by ¼" (6mm) all around. Be sure to allow extra length to follow the contours of the wire. Using 32-gauge wire or beading wire, stitch the screen cloth onto the wire frame. Leave the masking tape in place as you stitch around the frame until you get to the taped area. Remove the tape before stitching the screen to the wire.

12. Now you have a cabinet top (the screen) but no way to make it stay in place. To resolve this, you'll add two pieces that form a channel that just slides right on to the side walls of the cabinet.

Start by cutting two elongated circles about 2" (13cm) wide, from chipboard. (It's easy to make an elongated circle by overlapping two regular circles.)

13. Make two folds in the center about ¼" (6mm) apart (or at least as wide as the side wall of the cabinet plus some extra room for the clay).

14. Add a thin layer of mixed clay to the inside of the circle, leaving the areas where the folds are, free of clay.

15. Add a bit thicker layer of mixed clay to the outside of each circle and blend the two sides together. Add texture using a texture mold (while the clay is still wet), if desired. Fold the circles and hang each circle on the side cabinet walls, taping them to the walls with masking tape, if necessary. Allow to cure.

16. Attach the folded edge of the cured circles to the sides of the screened cabinet top using some fresh, uncured clay. Allow the clay to cure.

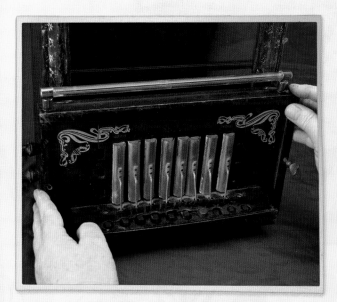

17. Attach a found object and some other embellishments, including crystals (see page 14) to the front of the cabinet to give the piece more visual weight and interest. (Add some scrap foam core if you want to protect the glass from the found object.) You can use clay or a different type of heavy duty adhesive to add the found object. I used part of a broken accordion to dress the front of the cabinet. I also wanted to add something on top of the accordion to catch the light. The glass rod, which I attached with clay, came off of a vintage vanity mirror.

18. With a craft blade, cut a hole large enough for an electrical plug to pass through the backside of the cabinet near the bottom. Insert your lighting element, art doll and/or other item(s) to display. Once you have an arrangement that you like, adjust the light with a safe distance from your objects. Secure the base of the light in place with some fresh clay.

Attach the lid by sliding the clay lid supports down onto the sides of the cabinet.

The Lantern Society
Lamp

The universe is full of magical things, patiently waiting for our wits to grow sharper.

—Eden Phillpotts (English science-fiction Writer 1862-1960)

I have a very strong connection to this piece because of a profound experience I had at an estate sale. The long version of this story can be found in the post entitled "Legacy" on my blog. I had never seen anything like the odd and unusual lenses I found at the sale. They were somewhat square-shaped and looked rather like faceted gems. Wow! These were cool! I brought them to the woman standing up front and asked about the price. She immediately lit up and said, "He loved these. He made these with his own hands, and I want you to have them."

This was such an odd thing to hear since I hadn't ever seen her before and couldn't imagine why she would say such a thing. She told me that she had a strong feeling that I was meant to have them. I found out that the things being sold had belonged to her ex—her daughter's father. He had used many of the same kinds of art materials

we do: found objects, ceramics and glass. Really a kindred spirit to be sure. Turns out that what he had planned to make for his daughter with these lenses sounded a lot like a design I had been working on for quite some time. I started to tell her a bit about the Magic Lantern and she was practically jumping up and down telling me that's exactly what he called it.

So I will do with this piece what he was unable to do before he died. I will make this piece and give it to his daughter in memory of her father. It's very rewarding to take a mass-produced rather cheesy lamp and alter it into something quite unique, and hopefully, into a treasured gift for a certain little girl who lost her father. As you'll see, only parts of molds were used to create the house shapes and they are all held together with wire.

Materials

found lamp

ornate gable- (roof) shaped mold

nonstick craft sheet

unmixed epoxy clay

18-gauge wire

wire cutters

acrylic paints

paintbrushes

8" x 10" (20cm x 25cm) printed transparencies, 2

printout of turbine pattern (page 125)

scissors

small diameter hole punch

stapler

craft glue

transparency of altered Victorian silhouette figures sized to fit on side of lamp

masking tape

glass windows cut from pattern

low-tac double-sided tape

old cardboard box

Krylon Looking Glass spray paint, 2 cans

assorted glass shapes, crystals and other embellishments

sheer fabric remnant

1. Plug the lamp in to make sure it works and observe how it works. The wire frame on the exterior of these lamps comes in several shapes, and you can adjust the steps to work with the shape of your lamp.

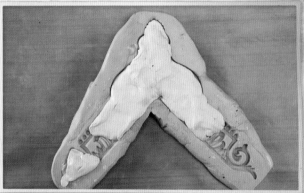

2. Sketch out the design of the sections you'll be creating. Create clay castings that can be used to build the sections of the outside of your lamp. Using parts of the mold will allow a lot of flexibility. Think of the individual pieces of cast clay as building blocks.

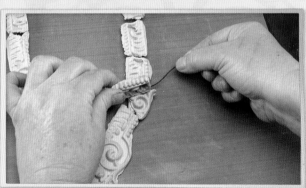

4. When each section is finished, adjust the wires, if needed, to align the pieces of cast clay "building blocks." Leaving some spaces between and making the pieces slightly different lengths will add more quirky handmade charm. Or, make them all the same size for a more uniform look.

Add a shelf by creating another section of clay castings. Leave a tail of wire on either side. Position the shelf in place and bend the wires behind the larger section. Secure the wires with fresh clay and allow to fully cure.

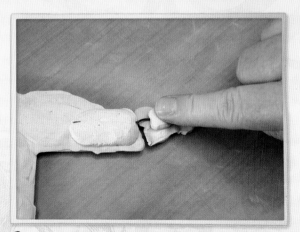

3. Attach the pieces together by spanning wire across the back side of two pieces and place freshly mixed clay over the wire. Allow to fully cure.

5. Paint the color(s) of your choice on all surfaces.

6. Tape the printed transparency with the allover design to the copy of the turbine pattern. Using scissors, cut along the solid lines and punch a hole in the center.

7. Slightly overlap each section by the same amount as the turbine on your original lamp.

8. Where the sections overlap, staple to secure. Remove the metal piece from the turbine on your lamp and glue it into the hole in the center of the transparent turbine. Make sure the metal piece is aligned correctly before gluing since the lamp won't rotate if it isn't sitting level and balanced.

9. Cut out a strip from the second patterned transparency and tape around the outside of the turbine with masking tape. Cut out the silhouette figures and tape them on with masking tape.

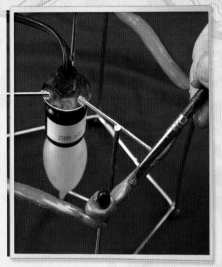

10. Center the turbine on the metal piece, onto the center "spike" on the lamp frame. If it isn't balanced, make any adjustments so that it sits straight inside the lamp frame. For example, you may need to add a little bit of weight to the bottom of the lamp in one spot. Turn on the light bulb to make it spin. (Note: It may take up to a minute or so for the bulb to create enough heat to spin the turbine. If it doesn't spin, then it still isn't completely balanced. Adjust the balance until it spins freely.)

11. Flip the lamp over and create some small shelves out of mixed clay to help support the glass windows. Paint the clay with the color of your choice, to match the rest of the lamp.

12. Create a pattern for the size of glass needed to fit into each section of the metal frame. In the case of an octagon-shaped frame, reduce the width of the pattern by ¼" (6mm) per panel to accommodate the glass fitting together at an angle. You can always fill in between the glass panels with clay, but it will take extra time to cut them a second time if they are too wide. Make an oval pattern mask that will create a window on each piece of glass. Tape the oval onto the center of the glass with low-tac, double-sided tape. Prop up the panes of glass in a cardboard box that is in a well-ventilated area, preferably outside. Apply several coats of spray paint following the manufacturer's directions.

13. Place the glass panes on the clay shelves. Tape them in place with masking tape.

14. Apply freshly mixed clay snakes between the panes of glass. Press in place and smooth with a small amount of water.

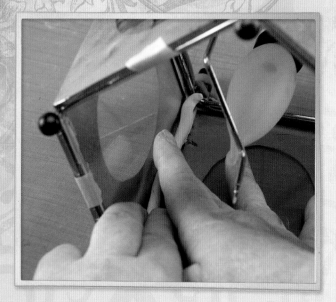

15. Repeat on the inside of the lamp to securely hold the glass panes in place. Allow clay to fully cure.

16. Remove the tape. Apply texture to the clay between the glass panels and then paint the clay.

17. Position the clay house-shaped sections over each pane of glass. Make a special wish for extra hands but be prepared to use masking tape to hold everything in place if no extra hands appear.

18. Roll out snakes of clay and push it between the house sections, just as with the glass panes, and paint.

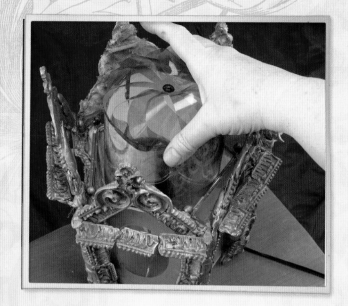

19. Insert the turbine.

20. Add crystals, elements from lamps and other interesting glass objects onto the shelves. The light will shine through them thereby sprinkling more magic about.

21. Plug the lamp in and take a peek at the little silhouette people through the windows; in a little while they will start moving.

22. Drape a sheer fabric remnant over the top.

Defrosted Flying Charlottes

Frozen Charlotte dolls have been all the rage for some time now. But since they are a finite resource I'm creating faux Charlottes that (I think!) quite convincingly pass as the real deal. While I was at it, I decided to set them free from their frozen origins. These defrosted little lassies have wings that actually work by moving a hidden wire up and down, allowing them to fly free at long last! I've also been partying with another series of all goth Charlottes. They are so fun, but, trust me when I say, these dark beauties are NOT your great grandmother's Charlottes!

The Sparrow King

The king lives in a sequestered reliquary, nearly hidden from view. He peers out through the thick, rippled glass through an ornate filigree shutter which obscures the curious glance of any casual onlookers. Further exploration will reveal that the shutter can be moved aside for a partial reveal, and when the key closure is unlocked the king can be openly viewed and even removed; it is merely a matter of knowing how. It takes several steps to open the locking mechanism designed especially for this piece: the pin is pulled from the shaft of the key, the key slides out towards the front and then the window can swing to the side thereby opening the locket. Even more secrets—the bird's body under the royal robe is epoxy and more astoundingly, the side walls of the locket are also epoxy that have been soldered to the back. Yes, you heard it first right here! Epoxy clay can be soldered!!!

Terrarium

I wanted an herb garden right in my kitchen so that I'm able to cut herbs any time of the year. This is my solution. The glass panels are "clayed" rather than "soldered" together, and since the clay is waterproof it worked out ever so well. The arched windows with magnetic catches are hinged (made much the same way as the Nightwing Evening Bag on pages 71-72) to open out for easy access. All the found glass elements are attached using a method I developed so no adhesive is visible. This piece looks quite stately on my counter and sits in front of the window so my happy herbs get plenty of light. From the feet made of glass insulators, to the tip of the roof, this stands a stately 27" tall and makes for a most unusual focal point (and fun conversation piece!).

Botanika

I made this for my amazing and oh-so-dedicated daughter, Sarah, upon the occasion of receiving her Botany degree from Humboldt State. It's made almost entirely of epoxy clay encased in electroformed copper. The wheel in the back spins to reveal five different botanical specimens embedded in resin. Each specimen is displayed in the focal point of the optical lens so as they go past they are magnified to show more of Mother Nature's design work. The beaded elements include crystals, seed beads, metal heishi and semi-precious stones in greens and copper.

Encrusted Bird

This free-standing shore bird, made entirely of Apoxie over a wire armature, is covered with shells from my beloved Oregon beaches. I wouldn't dream of using grout for this intricate dimensional work. Just like I used on the Sailor's Valentine (page 22), epoxy clay is so much easier for mosaics! Quite the dashing gent, he also sports a scarf of seaweed.

Resources

Clay, Clay Tools and Resin

Fixit Sculpt and Apoxie Sculpt clays
AvesStudio.com

Silpak RTV Mold Putty and Paste
Silpak.com

Polymer Clay
PolymerClayExpress.com

Diamond Clay (Heavy strength paper clay from Japan)
PaperClay.com

ICE Resin
IceResin.com

Colores Doming Resin
RioGrande.com

Transparent Amber Dye for Resin (not for use with ICE Resin)
Shop.Rings-Things.com

Silicone Clay Shaper Tools
CoolTools.us

Clay CleanUp Tool
KemperTools.com

Paint, Ink, Acrylic Media and Powders

Adirondack Alcohol Inks
RangerInk.com

Doc O'Brien's Weathering Powders
MicroMark.com

Pearl Ex Powdered Pigments/ Metallic Powders
JacquardProducts.com

Acrylic Matte Medium
DeltaCrafts.com, GoldenPaints.com or Liquitex.com

Acrylic Gloss Medium
DeltaCrafts.com, GoldenPaints.com or Liquitex.com

Diamond Glaze and DG3
JudiKins.com

StazOn Ink Pads
Tsukineko.com

Microbeads
Shop.MarthaStewart.com

Drywall Sanding Screen
3m.com

Modern Options Metallic Surfacers and Patinas
ModernOptions.com

Mod Podge (Découpage Medium)
PlaidOnline.com

Dorland's Wax Medium
JacquardProducts.com

Looking Glass Mirror-Like Paint
Krylon.com

Miscellaneous

Transparency Sheets
Staples.com

Uplight used in Reliquary of Fishes
Save-On-Crafts.com

Gloves In A Bottle Shielding Lotions
GlovesInABottle.com

Edison Style Light Bulbs
Bulbrite.com

Power Cord and Light Socket Set
OogaLights.com

Faceted Crystal Balls, Crystal Elements and Chains
CrystalPlace.com

Foam Core Board
Elmers.com

Nonstick Craft Sheets
RangerInk.com

Index

About Kerin

Kerin spent her "official" childhood in a magical place near the sea but has yet to grow up even though she turned fifty this year.

Her love of playing in the studio just for fun often results in surprisingly innovative techniques and ideas. As a heavy user and collector of found objects, clays of all sorts, metals, resins and optical glass (just to name a few), she makes unique art jewelry and small-scale sculptures. She also toys around with playthings such as her version of old-fashioned automata mechanical wonderments from the 1800s.

When discovering a new idea, one of the first things on Kerin's To-Do List is to share it with other artists. So you can find her frolicking about here and there, teaching live workshops and also online.

Her heart goes out to artists that struggle with being comfortable with their gifts or somehow not reaching their dreams of living creatively. One reason she feels she is here is to help others as much as possible in this area. So, of course, she meets artists everywhere who are—by some amazing coincidence—just rediscovering their penchant for art, abandoned long ago or trying to get past obstacles to artistic freedom. And, they share these things with Kerin, often not knowing anything about her.

As part of her quest to share delightful experiences with other artists, she launched an online community in 2009, MixedMediaArt.ning.com. She believes it will touch the lives of many artists.

Kerin left her software-development career a while back to relocate to a remote area of the southern Oregon coast. Living a much simpler life has meant giving up many luxuries. But it matters not at all because it also affords more time to just be and spend glorious afternoons on the beach in one of the most gorgeous spots on Earth.

Kerin lives with her extraordinarily artistic husband, Charley, and their two Miniature Pinschers, Solow (as in so low to the ground) and Hootie—a Katrina rescue dog that is now living the good life.

Her greatest inspirations come from other artists, especially those in her own family: the aforementioned Charley and cherished offspring Shawn, Sarah, Christine and Ben as well as only grandchild (so far!), the Amazing And Oh So Adored Kyle. She is also quite lucky to be named an honorary aunt to another truly gifted one, that being Master Finn, son of equally gifted Alicia Caudle of Portland, Oregon.

One of the most important things to know about Kerin is she wishes You, the holder of this book and reader of this page, the most golden of good wishes and generous sprinklings of unexplained happiness in the most unexpected of times.

Some men see things as they are and ask why.
Others dream things that never were and ask why not.

George Bernard Shaw

Discover more inspiration with these North Light titles.

Dusty Diablos
Michael DeMeng

Bring your artistic yearnings and sense of adventure along on a journey to the land of *Dusty Diablos*. Inspiration seeps from every page, and inside here you'll find: a tasty mix of ancient folk-lore (from the ancient metropolis of Teotihuacán to the miracle witnessed by Juan Diego); colorful pop culture (who knew that Western-Horror was its own film genre or that there's an entire island overrun with misfit dolls?); and informative art-making how-tos (like the Tricky Burnt Paper Routine and crafting your own Nicho). Join author Michael deMeng on an artist's pilgrimage south of the border and experience a culture as rich as it is beautiful and as genuine and down-to-earth as it is humorous and fascinating.

ISBN-13: 978-1-60061-350-0
ISBN-10: 1-60061-350-0
paperback, 146 pages, Z3606

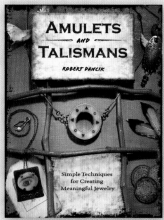

Amulets and Talismans
Robert Dancik

This in-depth guide is almost two books in one. Not only will you receive the guidance and insight to create jewelry that is embedded with personal mean-ing, but *Amulets and Talismans* also features extensive instruction on a wide variety of cold-connection techniques that can be applied to any style of jew-elry making. Incorporate found objects, personal mementos and more into one-of-a-kind pieces of art.

ISBN-13: 978-1-60061-161-2
ISBN-10: 1-60061-161-3
flexibind with flaps, 144 pages, Z2510

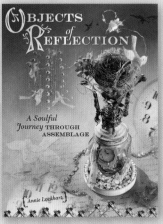

Objects of Reflection
Annie Lockhart

Objects of Reflection embodies visual journaling disguised in the form of dimensional assemblage by creating art that is so personal it resembles a page from the artist's journal. Inspiration pours from every page of the book through a gallery of projects designed by the author. In addition, more than twenty step-by-step techniques include tips for attaching elements with simple materials like string, wire and tape, aging objects, adding texture with mod-eling paste and more. You'll learn how to tell your own stories through your art as you turn symbolic objects into your "words."

ISBN-13: 978-1-60061-331-9
ISBN-10: 1-60061-331-4
paperback, 128 pages, Z2974

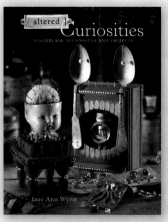

Altered Curiosities
Jane Ann Wynn

Discover a curious world of assemblage with projects that have a story to tell! As author Jane Wynn shares her unique approach to mixed-media art, you'll learn to alter, age and transform odd objects into novel new works of your own creation. Step-by-step instruc-tions guide you in making delightfully different projects that go way beyond art for the wall—including jewelry, hair accessories, a keepsake box, a bird feeder and more—all accompanied by a story about the inspiration behind the project. Let *Altered Curiosities* inspire you to create a new world that's all your own.

ISBN-13: 978-1-58180-972-5
ISBN-10: 1-58180-972-7
paperback, 128 pages, Z0758

These and other fine F+W Media titles are available from your local craft retailer, bookstore, online supplier, or, visit our Web site at www.mycraftivitystore.com.